Acknowlegements

In this book I have tried to cover many of the situations and areas in which people can find themselves tongue-tied and terrified. Saying thank you is one such area, so it is entirely appropriate that I should begin by expressing my personal thanks to the people who have helped to bring this book to life.

First of all, Isabel Atherton, my wonderful agent at Creative Authors who started the whole process. The many discussions we have had about all types of communication have been very useful in helping to shape the book.

Victoria Roddam, the commissioning editor at Hodder Education actually had the original idea for the book. I am grateful to her for allowing me to outline the strategies that I have developed and which I give people to help them deal with situations when they feel stressed and tongue-tied.

Robert Anderson kindly copy-edited the manuscript and made many useful suggestions which were incorporated into the text. Thank you also to Helen Rogers for guiding this book through the production process.

Finally, thank you to my wife Rachel for her continual support, and to my grown up children, Kate, Ruth and Andrew who had to put up with my jokes as they were growing up. Their collective advice about humour helped me to improve the chapter on joke telling.

Teach Yourself®

How You Can Talk to Anyone

Never be lost for words

Dr Keith Souter

Hodder Education

338 Euston Road, London NW1 3BH.

Hodder Education is an Hachette UK company

First published in UK 2011 by Hodder Education,

Copyright © 2011 Dr Keith Souter

The moral rights of the author have been asserted

Database right Hodder Education (makers)

British Library Cataloguing in Publication Data: a catalogue record
for this title is available from the British Library.

10 9 8 7 6 5

The publisher has used its best endeavours to ensure that any
website addresses referred to in this book are correct and active at
the time of going to press. However, the publisher and the author
have no responsibility for the websites and can make no guarantee
that a site will remain live or that the content will remain relevant,
decent or appropriate.

The publisher has made every effort to mark as such all words
which it believes to be trademarks. The publisher should also
like to make it clear that the presence of a word in the book,
whether marked or unmarked, in no way affects its legal status as
a trademark.

Every reasonable effort has been made by the publisher to trace the
copyright holders of material in this book. Any errors or omissions
should be notified in writing to the publisher, who will endeavour
to rectify the situation for any reprints and future editions.

Hachette UK's policy is to use papers that are natural, renewable
and recyclable products and made from wood grown in sustainable
forests. The logging and manufacturing processes are expected to
conform to the environmental regulations of the country of origin.

www.hoddereducation.co.uk

Typeset by Cenveo Publisher Services.

Printed in Great Britain by CPI Group (UK) Ltd, Croydon, CR0 4YY

Contents

Introduction

Talking is unique to human beings. Other creatures communicate, of course, yet we are the only species that has developed a means of transmitting our thoughts and emotions to other humans through the use of carefully constructed sounds or words. With over 6,000 different languages and dialects the 6.8 billion members of the human race live, work, socialize or disagree by talking among ourselves. We like and need to talk. Truly, humans are the chattering species.

Paradoxically, when you consider that talking is so natural to us as a species, one has to ask why many of us as individuals find aspects of talking so difficult. The fact is that while some people seem to be natural communicators, others find themselves tongue-tied and terrified in all manner of social situations where they are expected to talk to their fellows.

The reason is almost invariably fear. And right away let me tell you that the fear is usually anticipatory, meaning that it is felt in anticipation of some situation or event. The good news is that this single fact gives you *a key to unlock the fear* so that you can begin the process of overcoming it for good. I shall go into this in the very important first chapter of this book.

Many people are aware of this anticipatory fear: some experience it for a long time before an event while others just have it immediately before they find themselves in the situation. For some people that is all there is to it, since once they start talking they are able to cope and they may even give a spectacular performance. Yet others will not feel able to lose the fear and may find themselves tongue-tied and terrified. Some may even experience stage fright, in that they dry up completely and simply cannot talk at all.

If you have read even as far as this sentence then I suspect that you have known situations when you have felt difficulty in expressing yourself or failed to get your point across. Most people have if they are honest with themselves. You may have found it embarrassing, annoying or even depressing. It may have been in a conversation with friends or relatives, in an argument with colleagues, in a dispute with a sales assistant, a waiter or a manager, or it may have been when you were just asked to say a few words at some event or another. Even worse than all of these, it could have been when you were hoping to forge a relationship with someone and you blew it by saying something foolish or inappropriate. All of these situations are common in life and bad experiences can impact on how you feel in anticipation of similar situations in the future.

There are a number of confusing different labels that get bandied about with respect to difficulty in talking, such as social anxiety, social phobia and simple shyness. Some people would suggest that they are all particular points or levels on a spectrum of anxiety. I think that social anxiety and social phobia are matters of degree, but shyness is different, although there are undoubted similarities between it and social anxiety.

For now, suffice it to say that a social anxiety is fear or apprehension about a particular social situation. At its worst this becomes a social phobia, in which case the individual will probably do all that they can to avoid the situation in order to avoid the phobic fear. Shyness, on the other hand, is a state of reticence that may make you reluctant to put yourself in a particular talking situation, yet you will probably be able to cope if you are encouraged. The first chapter will deal mainly with social anxiety and social phobia. I will then look at shyness in more detail in Chapter 2.

The first aim of this book is to help you to overcome fear of talking in any situation, whether that is simple chit-chat and chat-up or the cut and thrust of negotiation, the dreaded best man's speech or even an encounter with the media. The first chapter is going to focus on this, giving you a bunch of keys and strategies to try out straight away that will help you diminish the fear of talking.

The second aim – dealt with in the subsequent chapters – is to arm you with multiple strategies and psychological insights in particular areas or situations that can cause you angst when you have to talk. These will be helpful to both the socially anxious and the shy.

When you think about it, good preparation is the key to all human encounters, whether that is a boardroom meeting, a first date, an interview, speech or a debate. If you are prepared, know how to direct a conversation, keep it going and bring it towards a conclusion, then you are more likely to reach a successful outcome.

In every chapter you will find short Key Point and Strategy boxes which will act as instant reminders of the important points and strategies that you can put into action in the various situations.

This brings us to the third aim of the book, which is also the ultimate goal of the book. It is simply to convince you that instead of feeling tongue-tied and terrified, you can seem to be silver-tongued and articulate. Instead of fearing and dreading situations, you will find that it is good fun to talk.

1

Tongue-tied and terrified

That is a forbidding title for a chapter is it not? Tongue-tied
and terrified! It implies that you simply cannot get your tongue
to articulate words and that the situation you find yourself in
is terrifying. Some readers will recognize the feelings straight
away while others may not be aware of such excessive anxiety,
yet they are aware that for some reason they just dry up, cannot
keep a conversation going and accordingly feel that they have let
themselves down. Perhaps they just feel a bit shy.

The good news is that both scenarios can be fixed. But before
you start thumbing the pages to find the buttons that you press
to take away fear, or the aphorism, charm or magic spell that you
would like to find and use to take your problem away, let me just
say that there is no such button, no spell. This book is not going
to promise something that it cannot deliver. Yet if you read it
properly, digesting the messages, putting the strategies into action,
you will find that the anxieties *do* disappear and you will find
yourself succeeding and transforming yourself from a tongue-tied
bag of nerves into someone that others perceive to be a confident
communicator.

I want you to start by being honest with yourself.

You are not alone!

Have you ever avoided a social situation so that you don't have to engage in conversation? For example, have you refused an invitation to a party, a celebration or even a family get-together? If you have, it is no big deal; everyone is entitled to feel a little anti-social now and then.

Have you done it *repeatedly*, though? If you have, that is a little more worrying. Think deeper and be honest: have you ever used avoidance behaviour when you see someone you know coming along the street? Did you pretend that you hadn't seen them?

If you have, how did you justify it to yourself? Did your inner voice tell you that you didn't want to listen to them going on as usual? Did you tell yourself that you didn't have enough time? Or did you make some other excuse?

If you are silently agreeing, then you know very well that the reason you avoided any of those situations was because they cause you stress. You avoided them because you cringe at having to make conversation. You don't feel that you are very good at it. And you hate to admit it!

Top Tip

People who feel stress about talking tend to use avoidance behaviour.

I suspect that you know of many people who do not have this problem and you envy each and every one of them. Why, you wonder, were they born with the gift of the gab? Why are they able to speak to anyone when you cringe at the prospect of having to pass the time of day with an acquaintance? Why oh why can't you be a chatterbox and be the life and soul of the party and every social occasion instead of the tortured soul that hovers on the sidelines praying for the moment when you can escape? Why are *you* the only one to feel tongue-tied and terrified?

These people are not more competent than you. They are simply less inhibited. You have learned to be anxious in certain circumstances, that is all. You can combat that anxiety and defeat it by using various strategies in the various types of talking situations that you will come across.

Of course, you may not feel that you have a problem as bad as this, in which case please feel free to move on to the next chapter. But, if you have empathized with the questions thus far, stick with it. I want to explain why I know which questions to ask.

It is simply that I used to be painfully, almost pathologically shy as well. Despite that, I have spent my life in medicine, talking to people. That has been a wonderful privilege, yet it has been daunting on many occasions. I have learned how to give bad news and to deal with aggressive and angry people and people in great distress. I have had to present papers, lecture to hundreds of people, and on occasion I have given radio and television interviews. I do not tell you this to demonstrate how confident I am. Rather I tell you because I have learned strategies to cope with anxiety, deal with tricky situations, keep conversations going and project my voice when speaking in public. And if I can do it, so can you. It is just going to be a matter of getting your mind to work for you instead of against you. We will have to silence that inner critic so that you can get out there and have some fun talking.

Top Tip

In any social gathering, the majority of people there will want someone else to engage them in conversation first.

A common social phobia

A phobia is an intense fear of certain situations, activities, things or creatures. There is a huge list of these, most of which have exotic names. The term 'phobia' comes from the Greek *phobos*, meaning fear or morbid fear. The thing is that the fear is more than slight anxiety; it can verge on panic and it induces a desire to avoid the situation or get away from the situation as quickly as possible.

The commonest phobias are specific phobias, such as fear of insects and spiders, and social phobias. A social phobia, as the name implies, is a fear of some social activity or social situation. One of the most common social phobias is a phobia of public speaking. The term for this is glossophobia, from *glossa*, meaning tongue and *phobos*, which, as you know, means fear. It is followed closely by a phobia of simple conversation. To put it into perspective, social phobias occur in one person in ten. That is a lot of people.

When faced with the provoking situation or activity someone with a phobia is liable to experience a fight-or-flight reaction. This is effectively a natural reaction to the release of adrenaline from their adrenal glands. This speeds up the heart, quickens the breathing, causes the mouth to go dry and butterflies to erupt in the tummy. It is the body's way of getting you ready to either fight or fly away as quickly as possible. You can imagine that in days when such reactions were necessary in order to survive this reaction would have been very useful. Nowadays, for most people who experience a full-blown fight-or-flight reaction, it is just unpleasant.

The result of phobic fear is generally to make people avoid the situation that causes them stress. Do you recognize that? If so, then, yes, you may have a social phobia.

Just butterflies

Perhaps it is not as bad as that for you. Maybe you just experience a little apprehension that manifests as butterflies. Or as a dry mouth. Or a queasiness in the stomach.

The thing is that it isn't an either/or situation, but is more of a spectrum. That is, the mildest of butterflies or the utter panic of phobic fear are all manifestations of the same stimulus; they are just a matter of degree. Social anxiety is much more common than a social phobia. Figures vary, but anything up to 60 per cent of people will have experienced symptoms at some time. About 40 per cent of people regularly experience a social anxiety.

In my experience most people when they are asked to assess their level of discomfort or distress on a scale of zero to ten, where zero is no fear and ten is abject panic, usually say that they would feel happier if they could at least shift their level down a few units. To have no fear would be excellent, the ultimate goal, but most would be quite happy to go into a situation with less than their current level. That is they feel that they could function adequately if their fear level was at a bearable point.

The good news for everyone is that you can always reduce that level to a bearable point. And in the majority of cases you can reduce it to zero.

What is it that you are really afraid of?

Now by that I do not mean that you have to delve deep into the recesses of the unconscious mind to uncover the root cause of the fear. That is one approach but at the moment it is not necessarily the most helpful strategy.

No, what I mean is what are you *really* afraid of?

The following are the commonest answers that I have been given:

> 'I'm scared of seeming stupid or inadequate.'
> 'I am terrified that people will see how useless I am.'
> 'I am scared that they will see through me.'
> 'I get petrified that they will see me crumble in front of them.'

All of those are interesting. But take that very last one. Look at what was said in literal terms. When asked to explain herself the lady said it was just what she felt: first she would be unable to move, as if turned to stone, then she would just be destroyed in front of everyone. She went on to explain that standing in front of a group to talk was her worst possible nightmare and it would destroy her as a person. She had sleepless nights for weeks before a presentation.

Note that! *Symptoms for a long time beforehand.*

That is a key feature that I suspect you can agree with. I emphasize that it is a *key* feature. I believe it is exactly that – it is the key that you can use to unlock the fear.

Anticipatory anxiety

In my opinion this is the very crux of the matter in 95 per cent of cases. People have fear in anticipation of the event. It gradually builds up as the event approaches, possibly reaching a crescendo just before it. Then quite amazingly, it often disappears when the individual gets up to talk.

Is that not amazing? Have you actually experienced it? The agony, the anticipation, is the problem. It is fear that you are going to experience intense fear when the moment comes. But in the vast majority of cases, once you are up and off, you are OK. At least, the fear is reduced and you then have to get on and perform.

I will come to the performance aspect in a later chapter. There are so many strategies that you can put into action there. For now we need to focus on getting rid of the fear.

Top Tip
Many actors, including the great Lord Olivier himself, suffer from anticipatory fear, yet are able to adopt a role that makes them appear fearless.

Which psychological model?

There is a good chance that you will have already read at least two books on various aspects of talking. I find that people who come to see me with a social anxiety problem have usually been trying for some time to find the answer, the method or the magic formula that is going to take away their fear. Although the books have seemed logical and may have helped them to some degree, they have not done the whole job. They may also have tried hypnosis, psychotherapy, Cognitive Behavioural Therapy (CBT), Neuro Linguistic Programming (NLP), or any of a dozen other methods, with varying success.

Once again, if you can empathize with this scenario and you are reading this book, you are still clearly looking for that answer. You want the removal of your fear for ever so that you are never fearful of talking again.

I am not going to promise you that I can get rid of that fear for ever. In fact, I am not going to guarantee anything. What I am going to do is give you a number of different strategies, each of which has worked at least for some people.

My advice is not to look for gurus. I am not one and I have never pretended to be one. I am a facilitator. That is, I help people to find the system that works for them. I do not use complex systems, since I do not believe that they are necessary. I use an amalgam of different models, schools of thought and techniques and as I talk to people I try to find the right one for the individual. There is no one system that works for everyone. Every person on this planet is unique – physically, emotionally and psychologically.

I do not of course have the luxury of being able to sit and talk to you. Indeed, if you can find the strategy that works for you then you will be able to solve the problem yourself.

Not one key but a whole bunch

People spend a lot of time looking for a magic answer to their anxiety. They would be better served by using a key that will unlock the fear. It may not let all of it go, but it will let enough out to allow you to function.

As you put the various strategies throughout the book into action, you will find that the fear does actually go of its own accord. Simply through you getting up and doing what you fear doing.

In the introduction I talked about a key that you can use straight away to unlock the fear. In fact, I am now going to hand you a bunch of keys (half a dozen of them, in fact) to try out. They all work, provided you understand the thinking behind each one.

KEY 1 – PARADOXICAL INTENTION

The simple technique called 'paradoxical intention' can make many people instantly lose their fear of talking.

There were three famous Viennese 'schools' of psychiatry. Sigmund Freud established the first school of thought, which was psychoanalysis. Alfred Adler established the second, which was based on 'individual psychology'. The third was called logotherapy and was founded by Viktor Frankl.

Frankl was a Holocaust survivor. In establishing his philosophy of Logotherapy he taught that we have a choice as to how we view things. One must work against a tendency to be pessimistic and to try to become an optimist. More and more research supports this view; optimists, for instance, generally cope better with illness.

One of the most important of Frankl's concepts was that of *anticipatory anxiety*. This is actually more than simply the fear that one has before an event. It is the anxiety about something happening, which is actually likely to make it happen. In logotherapy a technique of 'paradoxical intention' is used instead.

Take insomnia, for example. If you are an insomniac you usually go to bed and try too hard to sleep, the result being that you cannot sleep. With paradoxical intention you try to do the exact opposite. That is you go to bed and you try 'not to sleep'. You may be amazed at how hard it then is to stay awake.

Another example is during a hiccup attack. Instead of trying to stop them, try to make yourself hiccup. Offer yourself ten pounds to hiccup again. This paradoxical intention method usually makes them just stop.

So here is key one. Instead of trying to get rid of the fear, which is what most people try to do, by reading numerous books, having various therapies, taking drugs to suppress symptoms, you should try to feel the fear. Try to bring it to mind. Just try to imagine it at its worst.

Strategy 1

Put yourself into a mini-situation that you would anticipate with fear, and try to make yourself feel scared. You probably will not!

KEY 2 – FOCUS ON THE SINGLE WORST SYMPTOM AND NAME IT

Rather than just thinking about how awful everything will be when you are faced with a talking situation I want you to analyse it symptom by symptom. I want you to really *focus* on the single-most troublesome or unpleasant symptom. Is it dryness of the mouth? Palpitations? Fear that you will faint? Dizziness? Butterflies? Diarrhoea? The need to pass urine frequently?

Make a list of the symptoms if you need to, and score them on a one to ten basis, with one at the mildest level and ten the worst imaginable. Decide which is the real nasty, the one that you need to get rid of.

Now give it a name. For example, if the problem is a quavering voice then you might call it 'Quaky'. If it is palpitations of the heart, then you might call it 'Rapper'. If it is tight breathing, then you might call it 'Wheezebag'.

Next visualize that symptom, not in the effect that it has, but as a physical living thing. Quaky, for example, might be a cartoon character who is cold, shivering and quaking, unable to talk. The point is that if you visualize the worst symptom you have like this, you cannot be scared of it. If it is a Rapper, imagine it like a woodpecker, perhaps a cartoon woodpecker. It cannot scare you.

If you can visualize the worst thing, then you can control it, minimize it until it is of no concern.

Strategy 2

Think and name your worst symptom, visualize it as a living thing, or as a cartoon character, so that you can ridicule it, control it and minimize it. Put it in a cage so that it cannot get out and bother you.

KEY 3 – SHIFT YOUR FOCUS

In most situations that you are going to be called upon to speak there is a tendency to imagine that your part is more important than it is. That is, you put yourself in centre stage and your fear is unleashed. All sorts of thoughts start to crowd in, and you worry about how you are going to perform, and how people will view your performance.

No one will actually expect you to be perfect. The truth is that 95 per cent of people who give lectures, speeches and presentations do so less than perfectly. People do not hang on their every word; they do not remember what they say. They get an impression of the talk, presentation or lecture. They are not waiting for words of wisdom, but are waiting to hear whatever information you have to impart; that is all.

Do not think that they are there to judge you. They are not listening to hear mistakes. They will not notice mistakes or stumbles. In most situations people will either be indifferent to you or they will be on your side. You are just part of the process, not actually the process itself.

So make a mental switch. Shift the focus from your anxiety and fear of the situation and instead just focus on the message. Cut yourself some slack. You do not have to be word perfect; no one is. You do not have to cover every single fact, or tell jokes with comic genius timing.

Understand that this is not about you as a person; it is just about you getting up and saying what you need to say and then sitting down. If you can do this and realize that you are not the focus of everyone's attention, but are merely the messenger, then your anxiety will drop. It is the message that people are listening to.

This is not to say that you don't want to give a performance to the best of your ability. I will come to that in later chapters. The point is that you can alter the part you play. Instead of seeing yourself as the focus of the whole thing, you are just there to perform part of the process. There really is no need to be fearful about it.

Strategy 3

Start seeing yourself as part of the process. Just think of yourself as a messenger, passing on information. You are not the guru, the main character; you do not have to be perfect.

At a social situation select a moment to chip in, perhaps to thank a host on behalf of everyone else, or just propose a toast, realizing that as you do this everyone will be on your side, thinking what a nice gesture, rather than judging how you did. There is no need for them to do that.

KEY 4 – ACT

This may seem at variance with the last key feature, but that doesn't matter. It is simply a different key, leading to a different strategy. We will look at this in more detail in the chapter on performance.

Consider this scenario. A well-known stage or film actor appears on a chat show. You can see that he is uncomfortable as the interviewer probes him. Is it because there is no script? Is it because he is out of character and it is all about him rather than an invented person?

This is probably the case. Actors are people and they are subject to exactly the same anxieties and worries as everyone else. Many of them suffer from acute stage fright, yet they manage to go on and give inspired performances. But it is just that, a performance.

You may wonder why anyone with such an anxiety would ever choose a profession like acting, if it caused such angst. In fact, when one is in character, in role, the anxiety often goes. And it goes because you are no longer you. It is another way of shifting the focus.

I will come back to this matter in the next chapter, on shyness, because being shy is a highly misunderstood thing. It can be a great quality, not a handicap.

Strategy 4

Decide that the next time you are in a talking situation, you are going to take on a different character. You don't have to put on an accent or adopt a mannerism that is not you. You don't have to pretend to be a comedian, but think of a character who has no fear or anxiety. One of mine is to become a professor, the expert on a field, not necessarily the field I will be talking about, but an expert nonetheless. Spectacles help. In the chapter on performance I shall develop this in more detail. For now, just start thinking of a role that you can adopt. Your character is a fearless speaker and you become this person when you talk. Try it out in a mini-situation.

KEY 5 – PRACTISE THE THREE BS

This stands for Balance, Breathing and Basking.

Balance
Aim to be a balanced person. What you don't want to be is a cat on a hot tin roof, bouncing about looking nervous. Be balanced. If you look balanced on both sides of the body, you will emit the impression of poise, confidence and competence. The Alexander technique is a wonderful thing to adopt, aiming as it does to teach you balance. For now, all I would say is that you should try to achieve balance in your posture.

Try to get the muscles on both sides of your body as strong and as equal as possible. And that means trying to become ambidextrous.

Training yourself to become ambidextrous takes time and effort, but I do think it is worth it. Not only will you become more dextrous, but you will start using muscles on the other side of the body without really being aware of it. And that can only help your overall posture. That will make you feel more poised and you will become more confident, especially when you are in a talking situation.

To begin, start doing simple things like picking things up with your non-dominant hand. Use that hand to stir cups, to unscrew lids, to butter bread, and so on. Then try writing and drawing with the non-dominant hand. The results may be dire, but gradually you will improve.

Be aware also of how you walk. Do you initiate movements with your dominant side? If so, try consciously doing it the other way. When you dress don't put clothes on the same way, experiment, and aim at using your other side. Brush your teeth, comb your hair, put on spectacles with your non-dominant hand. There is no end to the daily tasks that you can start doing with the other side.

Breathing

Really, if you can get your breathing right then you have a simple way of easing anxiety levels and calming yourself down. I am going to give you three types of breathing exercise.

1 THE 4-7-8 BREATHING FORMULA

When people get tense before appointments, meetings, presentations and exams it is common for their breathing to become a little laboured and for them to experience some degree or other of anxiety. I teach people this simple breathing technique that often solves the problem before it has even begun. Just practise the following controlled breathing exercise twice a day, using the formula 4 -7- 8.

You can do this anywhere, but it is best to do it sitting with your back straight.

1 *Begin by putting the tip of your tongue on the roof of your mouth, just in front of your upper front teeth.*
2 *Hold it there as you do this whole exercise. Purse your lips slightly and exhale through your mouth, making a whooshing sound as you do.*
3 *Now close your mouth and inhale gently through your nose for a mental count of four.*
4 *Now hold your breathe for a mental count of seven. Having done that, exhale through your pursed lips, again making the whooshing noise, as you mentally count to eight.*

That completes one whole controlled breath cycle, in the formula of 4-7-8. You should do four cycles. And you should do it twice a day every day.

The position of the tongue is important, as is the sequence. That is, you exhale through the mouth, making the noise and you inhale through the nose gently. When you first do it you may feel slightly light-headed, but it will pass. You are not trying to fill your lungs to maximum capacity, or to forcefully blow out as much as you can. The whole process should be gentle. The actual time taken does not matter. Note that I say you mentally count the numbers. Each count could be a second or less. It is the ratio that matters, especially the exhalation taking twice as long as the inhalation. As you become more practised you can slow it right down if you want and breathe more deeply, but in the beginning it is just a matter of getting the ratio correct.

This really does have a tranquillizing effect on the nerves. At first you may not notice anything in particular, but after a month your system will respond and you will have a method of easing tension at any time. The important thing to remember with this is that you have to do the practice to develop the technique. So, if you only do this when you are faced with a moment of tension, it may not work. If you have accustomed your body to it, however, it will work.

2 ALTERNATE NOSTRIL BREATHING
This is another simple breathing exercise that is also worth trying.

1 *Press and close the right nostril with the thumb of the right hand.*
2 *Draw in a deep breath through the left nostril.*
3 *After taking a full breath, close the left nostril with the middle, ring and little finger of your right hand, taking the thumb away from the right nostril and slowly let the air out, expelling the breath fully.*

4 *Inhale through your right nostril.*

5 *After a full inhalation, close your right nostril with the thumb and release the fingers from your left nostril and breathe out through your left nostril.*

This completes one cycle. Just aim at three cycles at a time to begin with.

3 DIAPHRAGMATIC BREATHING

Finally, aim to be a diaphragmatic breather rather than a chest breather. Basically, there are two types of breathing – thoracic, where the ribcage expands and contracts, and diaphragmatic, where the ribcage is more or less motionless while the abdomen expands and contracts.

Chest breathers have an average rate of 12–16 breaths a minute, whereas diaphragmatic breathers need only 8–10 breaths a minute. If you do this you will literally save breath!

Start doing these exercises on a daily basis and, if you are a chest breather, then after one month you will automatically be a diaphragmatic breather. This will help you to be more relaxed and it will also help you to project your voice when you need to, as you will see in Chapter 5, 'Appreciate your voice'.

1 *Sit in a comfortable position and place your hands flat on your abdomen just below the navel, with the fingertips touching.*

2 *Now inhale slowly through the nose, at the same time pushing the abdomen out to make the fingertips separate. Keep the back straight to help the chest fill with air and continue inhaling for a little longer than you think necessary. This will encourage the longer, deeper and more efficient breaths.*

3 *Now raise the shoulders and hold the breath for five seconds.*

4 *Then slowly exhale from the nose and as you do so begin to draw the abdominal muscles in.*

5 *Let all the air out by exhaling more than usual, then when you think it has all gone, hold your breath for a second or two before you start to inhale again.*

Do this for five minutes once or twice a day. At first you will have to concentrate and you may not find it easy, but persistence will reap rewards.

Basking
This relates to the alteration in focus that I mentioned above. If you take on the persona of someone who enjoys being the centre of attention, then you can bask in being centre stage. That is it. Just start to enjoy the attention. Try it; it is simple.

Strategy 5

Start aiming for balance, start breathing exercises and try to bask in attention when it is focused on you.

KEY 6 – ALTER HOW YOU PERCEIVE THE AUDIENCE

Most people who have a talking anxiety fear their audience because they feel powerless in front of them. There is no need to feel this way. An audience is composed of individuals. Think of them as being friends, seek out the friendly faces and pitch what you are saying to them. Not just one, but several, so that you are interacting with the audience.

If you need to make them less powerful, then try the old visualization technique of imagining them sitting on small stools. You cannot possibly feel overpowered with this image in your mind. We will consider other things to visualize later in the book, but that is enough for now.

Strategy 6

Begin listing things that would make people seem less powerful to you, then imagine them in that situation when you talk to them. You need never tell anyone; it is in your mind's eye. The more humorous the better.

Summary

So there you have six keys and six strategies to think about.
Choose one to start putting into action straight away. There is
no problem about putting several into action. Nor is there any
problem about varying what you do. Your mind is extremely
effective and very versatile. Get it to work for you, and
demonstrate that these strategies all work.

Later we will look at other excellent techniques such as NLP and
CBT, which are also very useful in helping you deal with particular
situations and areas where you may dread talking.

2

Shyness

The reason that so many people have difficulty in talking is that they simply do not feel comfortable when they are the focus of attention, be that in front of an audience or talking with just one or two people. They feel awkward and self-conscious.

A lot depends upon who you are talking to, of course, because some people are easy to be with, easy to talk to and pose no threat. Yet the number of people that one is talking in front of can affect some people dramatically. Some people can chatter in front of a crowd of several hundred without any problem, while for others two people would be a potentially intimidating audience.

And the situation also will have a potential impact. Talking with friends in a bar or a club is less likely to feel threatening than having to stand up in a courtroom and be cross-examined by a barrister or other authority figure.

It is perfectly normal to have some nervousness before an event or before meeting people for the first time, but some people simply feel that they are being scrutinized, examined and tested. They feel uncomfortable and self-conscious in the limelight and may dread any such situation when they feel that they will have to perform in front of people, or when they have to make small talk with people they do not know well.

This is the sort of thing that a lot of people say when they try to describe their difficulty:

'I feel that people will think I am rubbish.'
'I know they will see through me, know that I can't think very well.'
'I just squirm, like a worm on a hook. I go red and want to sink into the ground.'
'I just don't like talking to people. I don't like the way I can't think in front of people.'
'I am just shy. I have always been shy.'

Can you see a difference between these utterances and the ones that I quoted in the first chapter?

The people in the first chapter people talked about how much they feared or were terrified by situations where they had to talk. The people who expressed the above feelings are giving a slightly different message. They are telling you that they dislike these situations because they feel uncomfortable. They may be able to cope, but they would prefer not to be in such situations. They generally admit to being shy.

Top Tip

Shyness is much commoner than social anxiety. Some shy people experience social anxiety, but not all shy people are anxious.

What is shyness?

In the last chapter I talked mainly about social anxiety and the specific social phobia about talking in public, be that before an audience or just making small talk with one or two people. People who are shy may be able to empathize with the feelings of social anxiety, without actually being anxious people. Shyness is different from social anxiety.

Shyness is more a characteristic of someone's personality. It is a state of reticence about facing certain social situations because they make the person feel uncomfortable. Rather like social anxiety the discomfort can be physical, emotional and psychological, in that you can experience slight jitteriness or sweating, some feelings of apprehension or your mind can go spinning off into the 'what if' zone. The overwhelming thing, however, is self-consciousness. This really seems to be the crux of the shyness issue.

For some people this can be an excruciating 'problem' to have. It can stop shy kids from answering questions they know, prevent them from asking for help when they do not understand and stop them from achieving their best. Adolescents often feel tortured by their shyness, finding that it prevents them from socializing, holds them back from presenting in front of their peers and perhaps causes problems in other areas leading them into trouble with such things as alcohol and drugs. This is important and we shall look at it in a little more detail later on. Some adults have difficulty with shyness throughout their whole life and because of it they may accept underachievement in many areas of their life in order to manage their shyness.

It does not have to be this way. In fact, there is much that you can do to counter it in order to overcome it once and for all.

How common is it?

It is not easy to get accurate statistics on this, because it is such a subjective thing, yet it is extremely common. About 80 per cent of people admit to having been markedly shy during their childhood and adolescence, to the point that it stopped them from doing certain things or stopped them from enjoying particular social activities. On the other hand, less than ten per cent of people claim to have never been shy in their lives.

The very first thing to note is that shyness is not necessarily something that people have all of their life. It is something that many people grow out of, come to terms with or master through the sort of practice that life throws at them. Almost half of all people who admit to having been shy in their adolescence will grow out of it by adulthood. This leaves about 50 per cent of adults who feel that they are shy and that this shyness causes them problems from time to time.

There are a surprising number of famous people in history, as well as current-day celebrities, who have admitted to being shy. The American presidents Thomas Jefferson, Abraham Lincoln and Theodore Roosevelt were all shy men yet they achieved the highest office in their land. The great eighteenth-century English chemist Henry Cavendish, who discovered hydrogen, was so shy that he even sent letters to his servants and friends rather than have to talk to them. Thomas Edison who gave us the light bulb and the phonograph was almost pathologically shy and Albert Einstein felt his shyness caused him great social difficulties. Princess Diana apparently suffered acute shyness when she was young. And, amazingly, there are many famous and celebrated actors such as Tom Hanks, Brad Pitt and Johnny Depp who are shy when they are not in character.

If all of these fine folk achieved great things despite their shyness, so can you.

Top Tip

Shyness can be an asset that will help you to achieve, if you let it.

Is it a disorder?

This may seem a strange question, yet it is an important one. The Diagnostic and Statistical Manual of Mental Disorders, or DSM, is a manual of diagnostic codes published by the American Psychiatric Association. Both it and the International Classification of Diseases, or ICD, published by the World Health Organization, contain numerous diagnostic codes for shyness in childhood, adolescence and adulthood.

But is it a condition? According to the criteria used in establishing these diagnostic codes, a condition is said to occur when it is causing the impairment of function of a person to some extent. That is not really a very clear criterion and it has the potential to cause difficulties for an individual.

Christopher Lane, a research professor at Northwestern University in the USA, has conducted extensive research about this issue, which he has analysed in his book *Shyness: How Normal Behavior Became a Sickness* published by Yale University Press in 2007. His feeling is that many characteristics and traits are now being medicalized, which is to the detriment of the general public. By labelling a characteristic like shyness as a condition it is being implied that it has a biological cause. This being the case there is an opportunity for the pharmaceutical industry to begin producing medication in order to treat the condition. Not only that, but if there is a diagnostic code or label, then this can find its way onto a patient's medical records, which could have an influence upon whether or not an insurance company would accept an individual at a normal premium, if they were perceived to have a condition.

I take the view that shyness is definitely not a condition, but that it is a characteristic of an individual. Further I would say that it is a characteristic that is not permanent, but which can be overcome, if the individual perceives that it is a problem. The thing is, it can be an asset!

The causes of shyness

It may be fruitful to consider some of the causes and see whether you feel you can relate to them.

First, it may well be biological. It may be in an individual's genes to have this characteristic. If your parents were shy and retiring then they may indeed have passed on this tendency in your DNA. This could have a direct impact on which neurotransmitters, the natural chemicals that are released between nerve cells in your brain and nervous system, are released and in what quantities. Effectively, your brain may be pre-programmed to function in a particular manner, so that you experience your dealings with people and situations in a particular manner. This does not, however, mean that it is a medical condition, any more than having an acute sense of humour is.

It is also possible that nurture rather than nature can have had an impact. If your parents or family were strict and you were always having restrictions placed upon you, or you were told that you should be quiet while adults are present, or that you should only speak when spoken to, then the seeds of shyness may have been implanted. One can easily see how this could cause one difficulty in later life when dealing with authority figures, such as your boss, policemen, lawyers and doctors.

The process of socialization, or the composite influence of family, teachers and peers upon us as we grow up, can also affect the way that we react and perceive things. If you had been subject to any type of bullying, were humiliated, browbeaten or excessively chastized, then you may well have developed a shy personality as a result.

The modern world is also said to be more likely to make people shy because there are more opportunities to avoid personal contact. Mobile phones, emails, social networking all offer ways of communicating without meeting face to face. This may be less threatening but lack of contact may mean that people do not develop social skills, or that they use them less frequently. While this will not bother most people, for some it may make an innate shyness worse.

And of course the various challenges that life can throw at one can affect one's equanimity. Accidents, physical, psychological or emotional traumas can all alter our perception of the safety or otherwise of certain situations. A hospitalization with an illness can make you feel more vulnerable, a broken relationship can affect your perception of yourself and your abilities, loss of a job, rejection of your work or of some offering you may have made to an organization or a person can all affect how you feel about yourself. They can all potentially make you feel uncomfortable about being in your own skin, so to speak.

Introversion and extraversion

The Swiss psychiatrist Carl Jung came up with the concept of introversion and extraversion. Extraversion is said to be the tendency to be concerned with and obtaining gratification from what is outside the self. That is, extraverts seem to be outgoing and enthusiastic and like to socialize, play games, talk and be with other people. By contrast, introversion is the state or tendency towards being wholly or predominantly concerned with and interested in one's own mental life. Introverts seem to prefer their own company and devote time to computer games, reading, writing and solitary activities such as meditation, fishing or walking.

People often mistake introversion for shyness. They are not the same thing at all. An introvert may prefer his or her own company yet can be sociable and good at interacting when the mood takes them. And on the other hand, an extravert can be shy. Take the examples of all those historical characters and celebrities who were/are shy.

Disadvantages of shyness

The most obvious disadvantage of being shy is that it prevents you from meeting people. If you have difficulty in making conversation then there is a tendency to avoid social interactions. If you avoid interactions you will not make a wide circle of friends.

Shy people tend to be self-judgemental. They tend to have a negative image of themselves and feel that others will tend to judge them on how they perform. Their own inner critic (and we shall look at the inner critic in the next chapter) tends to give them a hard time and is forever preparing them for failure in a social situation. Again, this will tend to make them avoid such situations.

Clearly, if you are not putting yourself into social situations you will not learn the art of conversation or develop your social skills. And an art it certainly is. We will look at this in many of the following chapters.

If you repeatedly fail to interact with people or avoid social contact when it is offered to you then people will form an opinion about you. They may think that you are unfriendly, when you really desperately wish that you could let yourself be friendly. Or you may come across as arrogant, vain or even a bit selfish.

Interestingly, shy people very often fall into bad habits, such as over-imbibing alcohol or taking so-called social drugs like cannabis. By experimenting with them there may be a tendency to think that they remove the shyness and so there can be an escalation of intake and the development of a dependency problem.

Social advancement may be a problem if you are shy because you are unable to let people see the real you. Shy people tend to have a problem talking to people in authority, so you may fail to show enthusiasm, shy away from discussions and be thought less adept and less intelligent than you are. It is common for shy people to underachieve in their careers simply because they do not push themselves forward. They may be reluctant to take on leadership roles since that will tend to put them under the scrutiny of their boss or manager as well as that of those they are trying to lead.

Advantages of shyness

Everyone should feel comfortable in their own skin. Being shy is not something to be ashamed of. As I said, there are ways of overcoming it, which we shall look at in the next chapter. But for now I would like you to consider that there are advantages in being shy. People don't always think about this because they are aware of some of the disadvantages that I have just set down, or they have heard that shyness is a problem and that you must get rid of it. However, instead of thinking of it as an impediment, a condition or even a social handicap, it is worth considering that at times being shy can be regarded as a quality.

In some cultures shyness is definitely regarded as a quality. In Japan, for example, it is considered a social attribute. Being brash is almost a taboo. The Japanese code of etiquette is ideally suited to the shy individual.

In childhood, shyness is a good thing. A natural wariness of strangers is a safety measure that most parents are thankful for in this modern world.

Although people often see shyness as negative, it can make someone very attractive. Instead of appearing to be egocentric, a shy person can be quiet, mysterious and appealing. People often want to get to know that alluring person, to be able to break the veneer or the shell and get to know the real person.

Shy people often do not want to initiate conversations, yet their demeanour may be non-threatening so that they are often sought out by others to confide in. Because shy people do not fill the air with aimless chatter they can be seen as people who listen. Indeed, the caring professions seem to have a high proportion of people who are shy in certain situations, yet who are all of an undoubted caring nature.

Some people use their shyness as a challenge to take on roles and put themselves into situations that challenge them. This is truly a way of making shyness work for you. And this is one of the main aims of this book – to help you to talk to others in all sorts of situations.

So now let us look at how we can set about overcoming shyness. One way is to silence the inner critic that makes life so hard for you.

3

Silence your inner critic

I do not propose to delve too deeply into the different schools of therapeutic psychology in this chapter. What I do want to do is show you that although there are many different models of the mind and many different therapeutic approaches, such as Cognitive Behavioural Therapy (CBT), Neuro Linguistic Programming (NLP) and all of the various psychotherapies, yet they all share one common feature. That is, they all aim to help people by getting part of the individual's mind to work for them, rather than against them. That part has been called the inner critic. In my view it is probably the simplest and the best thing for the person who has difficulty talking to consider. Effectively, we want to silence that inner critic.

What some psychologists said about talking

But first, let's look at what the leading psychologists thought about talking difficulties.

SIGMUND FREUD THE FOUNDER OF PSYCHOANALYSIS

Freud was a neurologist and developed a model of the mind that was based on the medical model. The psyche, according to his theory, consisted of:

- ▶ the super-ego, *the controller of the mind which acts as the individual's conscience*
- ▶ the id, *the unconscious instinctive and self-gratifying part that is like a mischievous little child, and*
- ▶ the ego, *or the conscious – the projection of the self, after integrating the drive of the id and the strictures of the super-ego.*

The process of psychoanalysis by free association that Freud developed works upon allowing free thoughts to be expressed, so that the individual can be helped to recognize their symbolism in order to resolve conflicts in the mind.

In terms of talking difficulties Freud felt that the individual experiences a regression to infancy when he/she feels vulnerable and subject to panics.

CARL JUNG AND ANALYTICAL PSYCHOLOGY

Carl Jung initially was a follower of Freud until he developed his own theory of the mind and his approach called analytical psychology. He believed that Freud laid too much emphasis on sexual frustration as the root of many neuroses. One of the main drives for the individual, Jung thought, was self-fulfilment.

He also thought that the unconscious mind was not simply personal, but shared a collective unconscious and that within it there were archetypal concepts that everyone inherits. He thought that these could be explored through dreams and the stories or narratives that people tell.

In terms of talking difficulties Jungian theory would relate this to archetypes. Essentially, we all feel vulnerable and are potentially surrounded by powerful enemies who know us and our weaknesses well. When we go into the arena we are exposed and our inner image will either allow us to perform if we feel strong, like a hero, or fail because out inner warrior is not strong enough. And even a great performer may occasionally fail, if his weakness or Achilles' heel is exposed.

ALFRED ADLER AND INDIVIDUAL PSYCHOLOGY

Like Jung, Alfred Adler also initially collaborated with Sigmund Freud until he went his own way and developed the second school of Viennese psychiatry, known as individual psychology. He felt that self-esteem was one of our main drives, part of which could relate to the pursuit of power. People feel weakened by powerful people and can become browbeaten. The inferiority complex was one of his concepts.

In regard to talking difficulties one can see how performing in front of people that we perceive to be more powerful than us can induce a feeling of inferiority and thereby fear.

VIKTOR FRANKL AND LOGOTHERAPY

I have already mentioned Viktor Frankl in Chapter 1, so there's no need to cover his theories again, other than to mention that the crux of his theory was that we develop anticipatory anxiety about certain situations. He taught that paradoxical intention can counter this.

We could go on to various other psychological theories, but these four leading thinkers in psychology give us enough to go on. You can see that they all indicate that in certain circumstances – and talking in front of people or just making small talk can represent such situations – we will feel vulnerable, defenceless and disempowered. In different ways that is what Freud, Jung and Adler proposed. Frankl suggested that we are aware of the things that will make us feel vulnerable and we magnify this in anticipation of the event.

No single theory of the mind has all the answers and, indeed, not one of them can be proven. As such they represent good models of the way that the mind works as long as one accepts the limitations inherent in each model. What we need is to find some means of unifying and making this complex psychology of the mind accessible, so that you can do something about your difficulty with talking.

The work of Drs Hal and Sidra Stone with their concept of Voice Dialogue is a good place to start.

The psychology of selves

Dr Hal and Sidra Stone are an American married couple, both practising clinical psychologists who developed a technique called Voice Dialogue throughout the course of their work over three decades. Dr Hal Stone had trained in Jungian analysis and Dr Sidra Stone came from a background in behavioural therapy. Together they became aware that everyone has not simply a personality, but a series of inner selves, each of which perceives the world in a unique way and which brings to awareness its own set of opinions.

Essentially, as young children we are vulnerable. We begin learning about the world, responding to parents and others by the development of a protector or controller self whose main function is to protect that inner child. That inner child is the vulnerable you and you carry it with you all of your life.

The protector is the first part of your personality to develop. According to your experience of the world, including loving parental relationships or otherwise, punishments, admonishments and so forth, you then start to develop other selves. The pusher is one that may enthuse you to do well, to perform, to achieve. The pleaser may make you amenable, willing and ready to help.

Two potentially very powerful other selves develop along with these. The inner critic who will keep you in line, find fault with you

and remind you when you are failing or putting yourself at risk.
And the judge, who will find fault and criticize others.

The inner critic

Of all these selves the inner critic is the one that can do the most
harm, especially in the way that you interact with the world,
although it is done quite inadvertently.

The inner critic is essentially the inner voice that is always with
you. Most people are not aware of it because it has always been
there, giving opinions, warning, judging and criticizing. It seems
to develop as a protective inner voice in the first place, in that it
stops you from repeating previous errors that had landed you in
trouble. Effectively it becomes a rule book that accumulates extra
strictures after all of the things that happen to us as we grow – the
knocks, the blows of life, the attitudes of parents, siblings, teachers
and authority figures. If it sees you heading in the wrong direction
or putting yourself in a position that it does not feel you are up to,
it will remind you of your inadequacies. If it becomes a very strong
inner critic then it may develop a very acerbic bite that will create
problems for you in various areas of your emotional life.

The inner critic is often involved in anxiety and phobic states,
depression, behavioural problems including addictions and self-
destructive habits or tendencies, sleep disorders and problems
with body image. It can drive the individual to distraction without
them being aware of it, and it can be at the heart of all sorts of
relationship problems.

THE INNER CRITIC AND TALKING

The inner critic is very clever. It should be, because it is an aspect
of you. It sees all possibilities, is gifted with an ability to work
things out to the nth degree, can go on the 'what-if' trail and cover

every eventuality in a matter of nanoseconds. The problem is that it tends to do so in a negative manner. Whenever your Achilles' heel is at risk of exposure it shouts at you to avoid the situation – you are bound to fail, make a fool of yourself and then have everyone laugh at you.

The thing is that the inner critic will have been doing this all of your life. You will have become used to the criticism and come to believe that you cannot do certain things, that you do not have the ability to perform, and so on. As I said earlier, it does this inadvertently, because it started out by trying to protect the vulnerable inner you, the inner child, from harm and humiliation.

When you were growing up it too was developing. The trouble is that it was taking in all the information that parents, family, teachers and peers were giving it, but it did not always get it right. For example, suppose your mother used the expression 'Trust you!' in the context of getting something wrong – 'Oh trust you to drop that glass!' This becomes literally ingrained by the inner critic to mean that you can't be trusted to hold it properly, but you can be trusted to drop and break it because you are clumsy. Similarly, if you often heard that you were a 'bad boy', then it can get interpreted as meaning that you really are bad.

If you had an uncomfortable or humiliating experience when you were talking in front of people, then that too gets recorded, twisted and fed back to you every time you find yourself in a situation where you are going to talk in public. The result is that you experience the anticipatory anxiety beforehand, it builds as you get closer to it and then you worry whether you will be able to perform or not.

You may have been involved in a conversation with someone once when you were told to be quiet, or you made a faux pas, were laughed at and felt humiliated. The inner critic stores all of these things up and uses them against you. It is done protectively, but over time it becomes so reinforced that when you are faced with a repeat of the performance it does its utmost to stop you.

Silencing your inner critic

There are really three parts to the process of trying to silence your inner critic.

1 RECOGNIZE WHEN YOUR INNER CRITIC IS TALKING

You don't have to wait until you are faced with a speaking engagement, begin right away, because it is likely that once you listen out for that voice inside you will start to hear it. Indeed, it is highly likely that if you have read this far into the book, you will have stirred up lots of associations about talking difficulties and all manner of recollections will already have bubbled to the surface of your conscious mind.

You may not actually experience your inner critic as an actual voice, but as a series of negative thoughts. Thoughts like:

'The last time you had to talk you felt sick and you had palpitations. It will happen again.'
'You have never been able to stand in front of people. What makes you think you can now?'
'Don't be ridiculous, you'll make a fool of yourself! They'll see you for the idiot that you are.'
'If you do it everyone will laugh at you. Remember how bad that felt?'

These are typical thoughts or inner critic utterances and pronouncements. Note that they are not just bland statements. They tend to be followed by a pessimistic prediction. In the past you may have reacted totally to this negativity and avoided the situation, or ground through it feeling that it was excruciatingly uncomfortable.

And it is very common for the inner critic to flash scenarios before your eyes. Like a teacher in charge of a projector he can flash pictures up, show you how badly things went before, show you pictures of the future and what will happen if you go against his advice.

It is an idea to get a small notebook and begin jotting down these utterances, flashbacks and predictions exactly as they occur. Date and time them. What you are aiming to do is to expose the critic, but not in order to get rid of him/her. You want to silence his/her criticisms. And to do that you need to start talking to him. (For convenience I am going to refer to this critic as 'him' from now on, but if your critic is female then modify how you approach her.)

2 START A DIALOGUE

That is right; you need to begin a dialogue with your inner critic, instead of just listening to his monologue of what went wrong, what will go wrong and his affirmation that you are useless.

To start with, try to picture what he looks like. Is he like a headmaster, a grumpy uncle, or like a gnarled old gnome? Bring him to life. You need to get to know him, so that he can see that your inner child has grown up. The role that he has been so accustomed to has changed. Instead of being a critic, you need to persuade him that from now on he is going to be your coach!

I suggest that you give him a name. Not a Mr, not a Sir, certainly not a Lord. Use a first name because you are going to be on a more equal footing with him. He needs to be your friend, not an authority figure who puts fear of failure and rejection into your heart and your whole being.

Now whenever you start getting the utterances and the predictions, challenge them. Ask him:

> 'How do you know that will happen?'
> 'Why do you think I will be sick? I don't get sick now.'
> 'Why should I be afraid of talking to them? I am a good talker.'

You see what I mean? Keep a little diary of your conversations. Record what he replies to your questions because you may find that the answers open up areas that you had not expected. You may find for instance that your questioning of him leads to him telling you that if you do go through with it and fail, that no one will want to be your friend again. But challenge him again:

'But why should that be the case? I will be with friends. They like me.'

3 GET HIM ON YOUR SIDE

That is right. After a while you will find that the sting of the criticisms goes. Then the criticisms no longer feel like criticisms. And eventually, you will have turned it round so that he will begin to work with you, to help you through the situations.

It may take time. He will need convincing. And he will start to be convinced when you stop manifesting fear. In the past he will have been adept at noting any hint of nervousness, but as you work with him he will help you to be confident.

In the following sections we'll look at some good ways of getting your critic on your side.

Making your critic work for you

USE POSITIVE AFFIRMATIONS

Over the years there have been many advocates of positive affirmations as a means of ego-boosting and getting your mind or your inner critic on your side. One of the earliest was Émile Coué, a French pharmacist and psychologist, who developed the concept of 'optimistic auto-suggestion'.

The application of the now-famous affirmation 'Day by day, in every way, I am getting better and better' is known as Coueism or the Coué method. It may sound rather banal, but it can make a difference to your self-esteem and will start to get your inner critic off your back!

Émile Coué noticed that when he was giving medicines to patients he could actually make them more effective by praising their effectiveness. This was the basis that he started from, and which he developed further by studying hypnotism. Good though his results with hypnosis were, he found that in fact the use of affirmations during full consciousness was often even more effective than suggestions given in a state of hypnotic trance.

He specifically aimed at getting the patient to replace the thought of illness with the thought of cure. In other words, he changed the focus of their thought from negative to positive. He silenced their inner critic.

Coué taught that many physical and emotional problems are the result of mistaken or distorted thinking. The imagination is a powerful tool when used positively, but a major impediment when used against oneself. If you can change that thinking and achieve balance then you can often lose the fear and cure your problem.

The main principles of Coueism are as follows:

▶ *Imagination is the principal force of the human being and is the language of the unconscious mind. Once the imagination is working for you there is no requirement for will-power.*
▶ *Imagination is more powerful than willpower. Everything that has been created by mankind began as a thought, as an aspect of the imagination.*

▶ *All thoughts continue until they have been discharged by action, or changed by other thoughts.*

▶ *Whenever there is a conflict between the imagination and the will, it is always the imagination that will win.*

▶ *When the will and the imagination are working together they do not simply add to one another, they multiply one another.*

So you see, autosuggestion or Coueism can be harnessed to silence your critic and get him on board to help you.

Strategy

By using the simple affirmation 'Day by day, in every way, I am getting better and better' you will start to get your inner critic on your side. Say it three times whenever you look in the mirror to shave, wash your hands, brush your teeth.

You can make up your own affirmations. In general, they are most likely to work if you precede them with a neutralizing phrase, and then finish them with an acceptance phrase. This is a method that is used in a therapy called Emotional Freedom Technique, which was developed by an American engineer called Gary Craig:

1 *To start you identify the problem that you want to work on and alleviate. Suppose it is a fear of making a speech.*

2 *Then you find the words that express exactly what you fear. For example you might say:*
   'I am really terrified of speaking in front of all those people because they will see that I am gutless.'
   Or if it relates to a specific person or persons then put them into the wording. For example:
   'I am terrified of talking in front of Dan and Karen, because they laugh at people like me.'

3 *Then put in the neutralizing phrase 'Even though...' (then add the sentence you had formed) '...am really terrified of speaking in front of all those people because they will see that I am gutless.'*

4   *Now you add the acceptance phrase: 'I deeply and completely like and accept myself.'*

    Note that this is acceptance of yourself, not of the fear. Thus:
    'Even though I am really terrified of speaking in front of all those people because they will see that I am gutless, I deeply and completely like and accept myself.'
    You just need to change the 'see' for 'think' and you almost have the specific affirmation for that particular occasion. The point of this is that it is custom made and because you have honestly verbalized what is causing you the problem, even if it relates to specific people, it is likely to strike a chord with you. The neutralizing phrase at the start will tend to minimize the impact of the thought and thereby of the emotion that it is linked with. The acceptance is all to do with feeling comfortable in your own skin.

5   *To complete it, we now need to add a further phrase, which relates to the fact that you are going to do and enjoy the thing that you have been dreading. For example,*
    '...and I am going to stand up there, perform well and enjoy it.'

6   *So if you put it all together now:*
    'Even though I am really terrified of speaking in front of all those people because they will think that I am gutless, I deeply and completely like and accept myself, and I am going to stand up there, perform well and enjoy it.'

    It might seem a bit of a mouthful. Write it down to begin with if you want, put it in your purse or wallet and look at it when you feel you need to.

As with the Coueism, say it three times in succession, whenever you look in the mirror.

You will probably become aware of your inner critic butting in to begin with. He will tell you that he doesn't believe it, or he will try to tell you that it can't work, it won't work, or that it is stupid. But that is when you challenge him. Ask him why it won't work. 'How do you know? We haven't tried it before. You don't know everything. It will work this time.'

Give that critic a hard time! Make him want to work for you. The amazing thing is that you will find that it does work for you.

Focus on the problem that really worries you. Be totally honest and construct your affirmation now. Start using it today, whenever you look in the mirror.

WEED OUT IRRATIONAL BELIEFS

This is also a good way of challenging your inner critic. This is by using techniques developed by the American psychologist Dr Albert Ellis in the 1950s. Ellis founded Rational Emotive Behaviour Therapy (REBT), which was the basis upon which CBT has been based. The essence of it is based on two things, reasoning and self-persuasion.

The reasoning involves looking at the way that we exaggerate how bad things are. A lot of that of course has to do with the voice of your inner critic.

Ellis identified a number of irrational beliefs that people hold. In relationship to giving a talk in public, people start with the irrational belief that it is important to be word perfect. That is just not true. Or that you have to cover every point in relationship to the subject. Again, that is nonsensical. You have limited time. Just the main points will do.

You may believe that everyone is going to be judging you. Of course they won't. They are just going to listen to what you say. They just want your message. Indeed, we shall look at this further in Chapter 7 'How you look, act and say'.

What you have to do is to dispute the belief. Tell your inner critic that he is not being rational. You tell him that you do not have to be word perfect, you don't have to give a wonderful performance, and you know that they won't be judging you.

You may find that you can put this into action by thinking of it as being as easy as ABCDE. Each letter stands for part of the process. A is the activating event that worried you. B is the false belief that was triggered by it. C is the emotional consequence that is triggered by A and B. That is likely to be fear. But the belief is false or irrational, as you demonstrate to your inner critic by D when you debate and dispute the logic. The outcome E will be an effective and rational belief. That is – that all will be well.

Strategy

Using the ABCDE, look at what event started your problem, then start disputing and debating with your inner critic.

BE AN OPTIMIST AND SEE ONLY POSITIVES

The inner critic is good at making you see the negatives. And if he has really done his worst he will have turned you into a pessimist with his negativity. Pessimists tend to have a lot of negative thought.

Let me give you four examples of such negative thought. These may be quite foreign to optimists:

1 They magnify and filter. *That is, they magnify the negative factors in a situation and filter out the positives. For example, a pessimist might complete ten tasks very well in a day, but one does not go so well. That is the one that preoccupies them and the others are filtered out and forgotten.*
2 They personalize everything. *A bad event is assumed to be their fault because of something they may have done, or because someone has reacted against them.*
3 They catastrophize everything. *They only see the worst scenario. Because of that they may adopt avoidance behaviour.*
4 They only see in black or white, never in shades of grey. *It is good or bad, more often bad than good.*

But all this can be changed. Challenge the inner critic; show him that his logic is faulty. Just because bad things may have happened in the past does not mean that is how the future will be. The past is not the same as the future and there is no reason why it should be unless you allow it to be. Use your mind. Instead of thinking 'I can't do this', think 'This is an opportunity to do well.' Don't think 'I haven't time to do this'; instead think 'I'm going to make time.' And instead of 'It always happens to me', tell yourself, 'There is no reason it will happen to me.'

See the situation that you have been dreading as an opportunity to change everything. From now on tell yourself that you are an optimist and that all will be well when you talk.

Strategy

Be honest with yourself. Do you magnify, personalize, catastrophize and only see in black and white? These are all irrational beliefs. Dispute them and start thinking not just in black and white, but in colour as well.

BE COMFORTABLE IN YOUR OWN SKIN

You have to accept that this is not going to happen overnight. Your inner critic has been working away all of your life, stopping you from being the person you want to be. But if you put these various techniques into practice you will find that the critic does become more positive and begins to take on the role of coach rather than critic. You too can start to feel comfortable in your own skin. Start to like yourself, appreciate your qualities and talents. Accept that you don't have to be perfect.

In later chapters we will look at some real strategies to help in the various areas that you might find difficult.

4

Hesitation and stammering

Many people find that they hesitate in the middle of speech when they are under stress. They believe that they do so because they cannot find the right word or the right response. That is quite natural, but practice will overcome it for most people.

Others do not just hesitate; they stammer or stutter. They have difficulty in actually articulating the words and all that comes out is a stuttering sound, or a repetitive noise as they try to make their mouths and tongues formulate the words. The more they struggle the worse it gets.

Simple hesitation and stuttering can suggest a lack of interest, lack of engagement, or show that you are anxious in the presence of whomever you are talking to. If the tendency to either is very acute then they can lead the individual to avoid social situations entirely. They can literally feel tongue-tied most of the time.

While it is outside the scope of this book to consider the subject in any great detail, I am going to give enough background to the subject to help people with a mild hesitation or stammer problem. If the situation is beyond the strategies offered, then it would be entirely reasonable for anyone with a stammer that is causing them difficulty to seek professional help from a speech therapist.

Whether you feel that you have a problem with hesitation and stammering or not, it is recommended that you read this chapter, since many people experience some problem at times, usually during a period of stress, so having an awareness of how the voice is produced and what things you can try to minimize the problem can only be beneficial.

Hesitation

The first thing to appreciate is that a hesitation or pause is not in itself a bad thing. Indeed, there are times when deliberate pauses or hesitations can be advantageous, but it is a matter of timing when to use them.

A hesitation in speech is a pause that occurs while one searches for the right word or just to consider how to answer a question, or phrase something in just the right way. On the other hand, if pauses are too long, then people will notice them.

Everyone does this from time to time, the frequency depending on a number of factors. Talking to authority figures, public speaking, situations where you are having to formulate things or if you are trying to impart certain information yet keep some information back, are all times when people may find themselves hesitating 'mid-chat'. It is normal and it can usually be improved by simple practice.

There is a game on BBC Radio 4 called *Just a Minute*. It is a competition between various celebrities to talk without hesitation, repetition or deviation on any subject for just a minute. Other contestants can interrupt if there is a slip-up, in which case it is their turn to continue, until they are interrupted themselves, or they reach the minute.

This is an excellent exercise to try in the family, or by yourself. All you need is a watch with a second hand or a timer for one minute. Open a newspaper and select a topic. It can be any single-word topic like the weather, trains, university, flirtation, etc. You just start talking, but aim to avoid ums and ahs, repetition of sentences and hesitation. You try to fill the air with your words and your eloquence for one minute.

If you do do this with a friend or relative as a game, you can have fun while you develop your ability to maintain a flow of words.

Top Tip
If you are a fluent speaker then hesitation or pausing are not bad things that you have to avoid at all costs. As we shall see later in the book they can sometimes be used to advantage if timed well.

Stammering

This is quite different from hesitation and can be a problem that some people seem to have throughout their lives. It is not a hesitation, but is an interruption in the flow of fluent speech. It can take several forms and can vary from a minor problem that is just regarded as an occasional nuisance to a major issue that can dominate someone's life.

About five per cent of children stammer, but most lose it as their language ability develops. Yet about one per cent of adults will retain a stammer. It need not and it should not stop you from achieving in life.

Generally, the term 'stammerer' is disliked and the term 'person who stammers' (PWS) is preferred.

Some famous people with a stammer

Demosthenes (384–322 BC). The famous Athenian orator reputedly had a stammer as a young man, which he overcame by practising talking with pebbles in his mouth.

Claudius (10 BC – 54 AD). The Roman emperor Tiberius Claudius Caesar Augustus Germanicus was an academic and scholar. His stammer and his clubfoot are thought to have saved his life, for he was thought to be a bumbling fellow who would pose no threat in the struggle for power.

Robert Boyle (1627–91). The chemist who formulated Boyle's Law and wrote the first chemistry textbook.

Miguel de Cervantes (1547–1616). Poet, novelist and playwright who wrote *Don Quixote de la Mancha*.

Sir Isaac Newton (1642–1727). Mathematician, scientist and Warden of the Royal Mint, and famous as the discoverer of gravity.

Charles Darwin (1809–82). The great naturalist who formulated the theory of evolution and wrote *Origin of Species* and *Expression of the Emotions in Man and Animals* (which laid the foundations for the study of behaviour and body language).

Sir Winston Churchill (1874–1965). Arguably Britain's greatest ever prime minister, Churchill was a man of many parts. Soldier, historian, writer, statesman and orator, he was renowned for his stirring wartime speeches. In fact, he admitted to having had a speech impediment all of his life and even had dentures specially designed to help his speech.

King George VI (1895–1952). This British king had a very marked stammer and worked with the Australian speech therapist Lionel Logue, who taught him breathing exercises that worked dramatically well, leaving him with merely a slight hesitation. An Oscar-winning film about this subject, *The King's Speech*, was released in 2011.

Marilyn Monroe (1926–62). An actress who could genuinely claim to have been a great film star. She had a glamorous life and a charismatic personality that led to her achieving iconic status after her tragic early death.

In addition there are many highly successful actors, singers and people in public life who have or have had stammers, including the actor Rowan Atkinson, the singer Noel Gallagher, the movie star Samuel L. Jackson and the actor Sam Neill.

If you look at this box of famous people who stammer you will see that many of these people were renowned orators. Their stammers could be overcome and did not prevent them from achieving great things in their lives.

The important thing to appreciate is that a stammer does not affect your ability to communicate. It merely affects the fluency of the speech.

COMMON FORMS OF STAMMER

There is no single stammer pattern. Each person with a stammer will have a form that is unique to them. Indeed, there may be no pattern whatsoever, the stammer being variable in both time and in severity.

There are three main stammer phenomena:

1 Blocking – *where one gets stuck on a sound or a word and struggles to get it out*
2 Repetition – *where one repeats a sound, a syllable or a word several times before being able to get into the flow of speech*
3 Prolongation – *where one holds onto a sound.*

Top Tip
If you have a stammer then pausing is definitely a good thing.

A mixture of mechanics and emotion

The fact that a stammer may be worse in certain circumstances than others implies that anxiety and other emotions may be a marked component in the stammer. This is more likely to be the case the older one becomes. It may even be a contributing factor in the development of social anxiety or of a social phobia.

It is worth looking at both of these areas now because if you understand a little about how speech is made then you can start to improve it. Similarly, if you can delineate some of the emotions that you associate with the stammer then you can start to deal with them, because it is highly likely that they are in a large measure maintaining the tendency to stammer.

THE MECHANICS OF SPEECH

As mentioned at the very beginning of this book we humans are the chattering species. Our ability to produce speech seems to be unique, although many other species are thought to be able to communicate sentient thoughts to each other rather than mere concepts of like and dislike. The means by which we produce variable sounds is complex and involves many different groups of muscles, all of which are under the control of the brain and central nervous system. In addition, we use our nose, mouth, palate, tongue, jaw, lips, lungs and diaphragm.

Air is taken in through the nose and the mouth and inhaled into the lungs. As we exhale it, as a result of muscle movement to contract the chest and diaphragmatic movement to expel air from the lungs, a stream of air passes up between two sheets of muscle tissue that end in cord-like structures called vocal cords in the larynx, or voice box. The front of the larynx is apparent in the neck as the Adam's apple, the prominence that moves up and down as you swallow. The vocal cords are a little like two small blinds that can be drawn across from the sides of the larynx to the midline. If the vocal cords vibrate then a vocal sound, or the voice, is produced. If the cords do not vibrate then no sound is made. The vocal cords can be opened, partially opened or closed.

The tongue is an incredible muscular organ that is used to grind our food, help us to swallow and modify the sound that comes up from the voice box. Anatomically it is made up of three extrinsic and three intrinsic muscles on each side, all of which are supplied by the hypoglossal nerve.

The extrinsic muscles of the tongue are muscles with attachments inside the mouth and jaw which help to move it around the mouth and help to alter its shape. The intrinsic muscles are contained fully within the tongue and their purpose is purely to alter its shape.

The different sounds are made by modifying the flow of the air stream that passes up through the larynx. This is done by variations in the shape of the mouth and the positions of the lips and the tongue. We refer to all of these as the speech organs.

A *phoneme* is the name given to the smallest unit of speech sound. These are divided into two types, *consonants* and *vowels*:

▶ *Consonant sounds – for example b, c, d, f, g, p, s, t and z – are formed when two of the speech organs touch or nearly touch.*
▶ *Vowel sounds – a, e, i, o and u – are formed by vibration of the vocal cords.*

To get a sense of the way in which the vocal cords function do these three things:

1 *Have a gentle cough as if to clear your throat. This closes the cords.*
2 *Exhale but make no noise. This opens the cords fully.*
3 *Hum. This vibrates the cords. If you feel either side of your neck at the level of the Adam's apple you will feel this vibration.*

You should now experiment with various sounds. You will find that many of the consonant sounds go in pairs – for example p and b, m and n, s and z, t and d, and k and g.

Note that the speech organ movements tends to be the same with each sound of a pair, but one is done *with voice* – meaning that you vibrate the vocal cords – and one is done *without voice*, or without cord vibration.

For example, with p and b, you need to touch the lips together and force air out of them in a little burst. The p is voiceless (without cord vibration) and the b is made with a voice or cord vibration. To test this make both sounds while you feel your neck.

Go through all of the sounds for interest and just see which are voiced and which are voiceless. The consonant sounds do tend to be made rapidly and the vowels are slower.

In speech we build up the various sounds to produce syllables and then words, which we formulate into sentences. A stammer may result when there is a difficult transition from consonant to vowel and back again. It does not take much to cause a block in the speech production. That can be a result of tension in the vocal cords, tension in one or other of the many muscles of articulation or even problems with the muscles of facial expression, especially the orbicularis oris, the muscle that forms the sphincter of the mouth and the lips. We shall consider these muscles in more detail in the next chapter.

SPEECH EMOTIONS

I am not referring here to the expression of emotion within speech, but to the emotions that can surround the process of talking and difficulties that may have arisen because of excessive hesitation and the development of a stammer.

The most common emotion associated with stammering is anxiety. People become anxious about situations where they are going to have to talk. Children who stammer may begin to worry ahead of an event and develop considerable anticipatory anxiety. Do you recognize this? It is precisely as we discussed in Chapter 1. Indeed, it is very common to develop a social anxiety secondary to the stammer.

In childhood and adolescence people who stammer often find themselves subjected to bullying behaviour from peers, relatives and, even worse, from teachers. This may persist into adulthood and people may find their stammer the butt of jokes from work colleagues.

As one gets older one's confidence can go, since many people with a stammer find that others lose patience with them and very often finish sentences off for them. This disempowers people.

Anger is common, although it tends to be suppressed and internalized. People with a stammer may become angry at others and their attitude towards them. They may become angry at themselves for not standing up to what they perceive to be bullying. And of course there may be anger at the stammer itself, as if it was a physical thing in its own right, a millstone that hangs about their neck and weighs their life down.

They may also feel jealousy and envy of people who are seemingly fluent and anxiety free. These can be difficult emotions to deal with, since it does nothing to help your self-esteem. It just eats away at your confidence because you subconsciously keep telling yourself that you are not as able as other people.

Common feelings associated with hesitation and stammering

- ▶ Anxiety
- ▶ Humiliation
- ▶ Shame
- ▶ Embarrassment
- ▶ Self-loathing
- ▶ Depression
- ▶ Suppressed anger
- ▶ Jealousy

The 'Life Cycle' and how to put things in perspective

There is a useful strategy that, if you put it into practice, will give you a way of altering how you feel about any type of speech problem. I call it the Life Cycle. It is a model that you can use to look at your life and the way that a stammer may be affecting you. It refers to the different levels or spheres that make up your life at any point in time.

There are five spheres or levels to consider in your life:

1 The actual symptom – *the stammer or hesitation.*
2 Emotions – *how it makes you feel, e.g. anxious, sad, depressed, angry or jealous of others who are not affected.*
3 Mind – *how it affects the type of thoughts you have, e.g. pessimistic thoughts, negative thoughts, self-defeating thoughts.*
4 Behaviour – *how it makes you behave or act, e.g. isolating yourself by avoiding things or people.*
5 Lifestyle – *how it affects your ability to do things, your relationships, and also how events in your life impact on you.*

Take a look at Figure 4.1. You will see the five spheres starting with the physical symptom, the body symptom – that is, the stammer – at the top. If you follow it clockwise you will see that it follows the order that I mentioned above – body, emotions, mind, behaviour and lifestyle. Note the outer circle that encloses the whole structure. This represents the individual's whole self, their life. In other words, the five spheres all make up part of your experience of life.

Notice also that there are double-headed arrows between the spheres. The outer arrows represent the general progression, because the order represents the way that a condition will tend to impact on you. The stammer or hesitation will have an emotional effect. This in turn makes you think in a particular way. The condition may come to dominate your thoughts – you worry about how it will make people feel about you, and how it will affect your ability to talk in public, apply for jobs, or even have a relationship. This can affect your behaviour in that you may stop doing certain things.

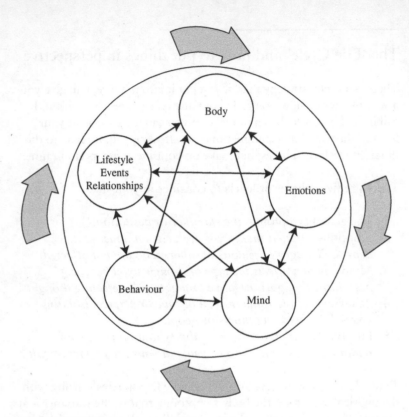

Figure 4.1 The Life Cycle.

It is so common for people with a stammer to use avoidance behaviour. This can be total avoidance of speaking, or the use of specific avoidance means of coping. For example, you may use alternative words to ones that you commonly get stumped on. Or you may feel that you can never get involved in debates, arguments or discussions for fear that the stammer will be triggered off. And this may affect your lifestyle, your occupation and your relationships. And, again, this may intensify the stammer.

Again notice the inner double-headed arrows – these represent the ways that the different spheres are affected by the other spheres. Indeed, each sphere is potentially affected by all of the others. This is very important, because the double-headed arrows also indicate that you have multiple potential ways in which you can affect the stammer. The problem is that it is so very easy to focus on a stammer as if it is the most important thing in your life, impacting on everything else. Viewed this way, however, if you feel a particular emotion, rather than allowing the flow of thought to be swayed by that emotion, you can deliberately try to introduce a different emotion. Or instead of allowing it to make you behave in a particular way, decide to do something different, though preferably something that is not the easy way out. If you get into the habit of challenging the reaction you feel, you will find that you can alter the way you feel, the way you think and the way that you behave. All of this will help you to achieve better overall balance in your life.

The point is that you do not just use this technique once, but use it whenever you find that you have a problem. For example, imagine you are about to go to the first meeting of a new club you have joined or to meet a prospective partner's family. If you find that the stammer becomes apparent or you have begun to feel anxious, rather than allow yourself to follow the cycle and start to think negative thoughts, you select a different sphere, such as behaviour, and do something different.

You may in usual circumstances start plotting how to avoid the situation, or devise some method in which you can merge into the background. This time think of what behaviour you could adopt to make yourself stand out. Or you go back a step to the thinking sphere and change the thoughts to something else. Get humorous – how could you do or say something funny. Be creative – remember to challenge everything and you will be surprised at how your thinking, your emotions and the things you do will alter.

As that happens, you will focus less on the stammer and hesitation and they will be less likely to occur.

Common hesitation or stammering behaviours

Avoidance of...

▶ *talking*
▶ *discussions or arguments*
▶ *telephone conversations*
▶ *meetings*
▶ *relationships*

Or people might...

▶ *adopt an arrogant or off-putting manner so you don't have to talk*
▶ *postpone things and never get round to them*
▶ *pretend that you think differently so you don't have to talk to justify yourself*
▶ *agree with others even when you really disagree so that you don't have to risk expressing yourself and stammering*
▶ *pretend that you don't have a stammer*

Most of the usual coping mechanisms that people who stammer adopt tend to be self-defeating. For example, they pretend that they don't have a stammer when they clearly do. You would be better to acknowledge that there is a problem and use different strategies to deal with it. And one of the most profitable things that you can do is to seek professional help. Your family doctor may be able to advise you on this.

You may also find it useful to contact one of the support organizations such as the British Stammering Association (www. stammering.org)

Stammer More Easily *or* Speak More Fluently

These are the names of two different approaches which are used by speech therapists to help people who stammer. They were described by Professor Hugo Gregory, himself a stammerer in his 1979 book *Controversies about Stuttering Theories*.

The *Stammer More Easily* approach is built around acknowledging that a stammer is a complex problem with both mechanical aspects and many associated negative ideas and feelings. The aim is to reduce the negativity and the tendency to use avoidance behaviour.

The *Speak More Fluently* approach tends to be more related to the actual mechanics of voice and speech production.

Both are extremely effect when used with a speech therapist.

SOME SIMPLE STRATEGIES

If you have no way of accessing speech therapy then the following simple strategies are worth applying.

Strategy: *Slow the flow*

The average rate of speech for an adult is 120–160 words per minute. People who stammer often speak faster than this, until they start stammering. The unconscious desire is always to get to the end of the sentence, so they speed up. The very rate at which they speak may be a trigger, because it demands rapid change between vowels and consonants, so that one can end up with a repetition or hit a block.

Slowing down is a good thing to aim at. A good way of doing this is literally to time yourself as you read out loud. Get a good book and count out the number of words per page. If the page is 360 words on average, then you want to try to take three minutes to read it out loud. That would give you a speech rate of 120.

This may dramatically reduce or remove a stammer.

Strategy: *Don't worry about hesitations*

If you are someone who has a stammer then pausing during speech is a good thing. Fluent speakers can try to reduce their hesitations by the exercise I mentioned at the start of this chapter, but if you have a stammer, you probably have a tendency not to pause at all. This may be because you feel a need to get your words out as quickly as possible. Instead of doing this, try introducing pauses into your speech. Don't stop mid-sentence, but try pausing and taking a breath after every second sentence. By doing this you are effectively taking the pressure off yourself, which is one of the things you need to do.

Strategy: *Maintain eye contact*

I am going to talk at length about the importance of eye contact in Chapters 6 and 7 on 'Small talk matters' and 'How you look, act and say'. It is fundamentally important in all aspects of talking and it is doubly so if you tend to stammer.

People who stammer tend to break eye contact as soon as a stammer manifests itself. The problem with this is that it reinforces the behaviour each time you do it. If you make yourself maintain that eye contact then you are automatically challenging the behaviour associated with the stammer. The more you do this, the more you start to lay down a new behaviour which is more likely to help you achieve fluent speech.

5

Appreciate your voice

Consider two situations.

Firstly, have you ever attended a lecture or listened to a speech and had to struggle to hear the speaker? People who are not used to making presentations do not always articulate their words properly or project their voice enough. It is not surprising, of course, since it is not something that people tend to practise.

Microphone systems should help, but they are not always reliable. A previous speaker may have fiddled with it, or it may be attached to a lectern so that the next speaker ends up hunched over the mouthpiece like a praying mantis. Worse, if the system unexpectedly packs up then the speaker is left to their own devices. This can result in an inaudible performance that is heard only by a select few at the front of the hall. On the other hand, someone may boldly cry out that the speaker is mumbling, with the result that a nervous speaker may just start to croak and bluster, or they screech as they attempt to shout their message to the rear of the hall.

If you yourself have actually found yourself in that situation as a speaker then you may have vowed never to speak in public again, or you may have muddled through, then done nothing to improve your technique and resolved to just get through it as best you can if you ever have to have a repeat performance.

The second situation relates to the other end of the talking spectrum – simple day-to-day conversation. Have you ever had to strain your ears to hear someone talking? You may have had to ask them to speak up a little because you can't hear. What happens then is that they raise their voice for a few sentences or exchanges, then revert to their soft whispering pattern. It can be very frustrating.

Indeed, most people can recollect such a situation in real life. When you experienced it what sort of emotions did it stir? Irritation? Embarrassment? Or did it make you want to get the conversation over and get away?

When people mumble they are giving out a message that they are not comfortable talking and they unconsciously make a demand on other people to lean forward and make a concerted effort to hear them.

Perhaps, though, you relate to the mumbler? If you can, it is almost a certainty that you have at some stage in life felt insecure in your ability to talk. You may have improved that, yet you will have retained that quiet, whisper-like tone. It is quite likely that you do not like the sound of your voice.

The key to avoiding these situations is to practise. Everyone can learn to project their voice and no one needs to mumble. In this chapter we shall look at some very simple techniques and strategies to develop your ability to project your voice with some confidence. It will simply require a little practice that you can do in the comfort of your own home.

Why you should learn to like your own voice

Self-esteem is very important. In order to enjoy life you should make it an aim to feel good about yourself. That does not mean that you have to groom yourself to look like a celebrity, or that you should spend excessive amounts of money on expensive clothes, cosmetics or accessories of some sort or another. It is about feeling comfortable in your own skin.

Your voice is one of your main ways of interacting with other people. It is your voice that will register with others and it is the way that you speak that they will remember. A good confident, clear voice will always stand you in good stead.

It is strange that so many people hate the sound of their own voice. When they hear a recording of it they often cringe and cannot believe that it belongs to them. The reason is that it sounds different from the voice that they normally hear. That is a fact. No one hears their own voice in the same way that others do. This is because we hear by two different mechanisms.

In order to explain this you need to know the way in which the ear works. We tend to consider the human ear as having three parts. The outer ear consists of the *pinna* (also called the auricle) and the *ear canal*. The function of this is to collect sound waves and direct them down the canal towards the eardrum. You instinctively enhance the effect of the pinna when you cup a hand round your ear to hear better.

The middle ear consists of the *eardrum*, the three little *ossicle* bones (*malleus, incus and stapes*; respectively hammer, anvil and stirrup, after their shapes) and the *Eustachian tube* which links this chamber with the back of the throat. The Eustachian tube has the function of equalizing the pressure in the middle ear with the outside atmosphere. The function of the middle ear is to transmit the vibrations on the eardrum through the ossicles to vibrate the *oval window* of the inner ear. They effectively amplify the sound.

The inner ear consists of the bony labyrinth. It has two parts – the *cochlea*, or the organ of hearing, which is shaped like a snail's shell, and the *semi-circular canals*, which help us to balance. The acoustic nerve is the eighth cranial nerve. It relays information about hearing from the cochlea and about balance from the semicircular canals to the brain.

The first hearing mechanism is by air and nerve transmission. This is the most efficient mechanism. It happens pretty much as I have already described, by the sound waves entering the pinna and being transmitted via the vibration of the eardrum, then via the bony ossicles to the cochlea, and then to the nerve of hearing which transmits signals to the brain.

The second mechanism is by conduction. This occurs when sounds are directly transmitted through the bones and tissues of the head directly to the cochlea.

Every time you talk you will hear your own voice by both mechanisms. Mainly it will be by direct conduction rather than by the air transmission by which you hear other people. It is therefore slightly distorted and will never be the same as when you hear your voice played back to you from a recorder. When you hear a recording of your voice you will only hear the air and nerve transmission, because the conductive transmission will be absent. This will tend to make it sound higher in pitch than you normally hear it.

That does not mean that it does not sound good! It does, because it is the sound that you make. You just need to get used to the fact that it doesn't sound the same as you have been used to hearing it.

Distinctive voices

What makes a voice stand out? Just think about it for a moment. What is it that makes a voice sound sexy to you? Or funny? Or powerful?

Think about people who have distinctive voices that you can associate with each of those qualities. Are they people you know or are they people you have seen on movies or TV chat shows, or whom you have heard on the radio?

When most people are asked this they bring to mind famous people from screen, stage or radio. Actors or personalities of some sort or another. And according to the 7%–38%–55% rule of thumb, which we will look at it the next chapter, the actual content of their speech, or what they say, will have less impact than how they say it and how they look when they said it.

Actors are of course excellent at making their voice fit a character. It seems as if they can almost do it at will, as if they had been born with that skill, which of course they have not. It is a skill that they have learned and fine-tuned through constant practice. When you hear actors perform on the radio this skill is really brought to the fore. They can create an image of a character through the sound of their voice alone and they can be extremely persuasive.

I will discuss strategies that you can use in persuasive speech later in the book. For now all I want to impress upon you is the fact that research has shown that when only the voice is heard, such as on the radio, the persuasive impact tends to come mainly from the way the voice delivers the message. It is the tone of the voice and the way that it rises and falls as the speaker conveys their enthusiasm to the listener.

Going back to your own voice it is a good thing to actually listen to yourself. This comes down to practice yet again. Simply get a tape recorder and tape yourself reading both fiction and non-fiction. Then play it back and listen.

Strategy

1 Get a tape-recorder, a clock and a couple of books. The first book should be a piece of fiction by an author that you find exciting. It should have lots of dialogue in it. The second should be a how-to manual of some sort. This should be a no-nonsense type of book on a subject that is outside your usual sphere of interest.

2 Record yourself reading for three minutes from the fiction book.Then without listening to the fiction piece, record three minutes of you reading from the manual.

3 Now listen to each and assess how excited you were by the reading. Ask yourself how well you were able to engage your own interest and how well you managed to convey a sense of drama and narrative with the fiction, and of interest and enthusiasm with the manual.

4 Then repeat the whole process, trying to read like an actor to bring the fiction alive, and like a TV or radio presenter who wants to fire your interest in the non-fiction piece.

It does not matter how silly you feel, this is an excellent exercise for trying to instil a sense of enthusiasm and passion into your voice.

Change your tone at will

The tone of voice that you use imparts a great deal of information. It puts feeling into your words, so that whomever you are talking to will perceive the more subtle attitude that you are trying to convey. They will appreciate whether you are talking seriously, humorously, authoritatively or enthusiastically. By being able to alter your tone you will become a better communicator.

Strategy: *Use a key word*

You can choose a word that can convey a different meaning just by altering the tone. For example, you could use the word 'please'. Try it out yourself; just experiment with altering the tone that you might use when you are exasperated, grateful, happy, or angry.

Another word that works for me is 'experiment'. Depending upon the type of talk, whether it is to adults or children, the tone in which you say the word can affect the mood that you are trying to create.

Suppose you are talking to a group of children. When you use the word 'experiment' you would say it in a friendly, cheery manner. The aim would be to create a cosy, atmosphere of wonderment. Then say it in a more adult, controlling manner. 'Let us try and experiment!' Here you would be trying to be forceful or hypnotic, and aiming to bend their mind to your will. Try it in a scholarly, intellectual manner, as if you are revealing an extremely clever new development that no one would have expected. 'As a result of our experiment, I can reveal...'

Change the tone that you use to say your key word and you can use that change to get the tone of voice that you need to use for the type of talking you need to do for the audience you are speaking to.

Strategy: *Picture your audience*

Your imagination is one of your best tools in your preparation for any kind of talking.

Whenever you are practising in front of a mirror or with a tape-recorder or video, get the audience firmly in your mind. Is it a friendly audience, a businesslike audience, or a group of students? Always picture them and use people that you know who have a particular type of outlook or personality that would fit that imagined audience. Cheerful people, or actual business folk you know, or students or schoolchildren you studied with when you were their age. Have them in your mind's eye as you give your prepared talk.

Pitch the tone you need to empathize with them. They won't bite, and your practice will ensure that when you come to talk in actuality, neither will the real audience!

Strategy: *Practise some patter*

Patter is a prearranged scripting of what you are going to say. It is not a whole speech, but the essence of it. The point again is that you choose the tone of voice that you need in order to deliver it appropriately. If you have the first sentence or two in your mind, practised so that they slip out naturally, then the tone adjustment is made effortlessly.

Imagine you are a conjurer:

'Boys and girls, I want to tell you a story about a time when I was the sheriff of Deadwood Gulch in America...'

And again:

'Ladies and gentlemen, I would like to take you on a journey into the convoluted regions of the mind. I want to consider the possibility of one person being able to read the mind of another...'

And finally:

'Hey, guys, do you reckon you can spot a cardsharp at work?...'

These three scenarios relate to a conjurer for children, a mentalist for adults and a street performer. You would not use the same tone for all three. You pitch according to the audience and the circumstance.

Choose a talking event that is going to come up, be it a speech, mingling at a party or just seeing your Aunt Florie for tea. Work out a couple of lines of patter and practise them in the mirror, selecting the right tone.

Adapt this to all talking practice.

Strategy: *Learn how to tell a joke*

This is not flippant advice. I am actually going to discuss this in a later chapter. I mention it here because a good joke depends on the way that you tell it, with focus on timing, the use of the pause and speed of flow. Master two or three jokes, which once again are based on good patter, and you will understand the importance of tone.

Now there are a few important things to consider about voice protection and voice projection.

Voice problems

You may not feel that you need to protect your voice. You may not be an actor, a singer, a town crier or a teacher. You may not feel that the amount you talk is likely to strain your voice or cause any problem. In fact, that is not true. Everyone should protect their voice if they use it on a daily basis. But first, what are the things that can go wrong with the voice?

Dysphonia means 'disorder of the voice,' from the Greek *dys*, meaning 'bad, abnormal or difficult', and *phonia*, meaning 'of the voice'. It is really a blanket term for a group of symptoms in which one has difficulty in talking or whispering, so that it may be painful to talk, hard to project your voice, or that the sound of your voice may have changed. One may almost lose the voice.

Voice problems are very common and it is estimated that the cost to the British economy is approximately £200 million a year, because people can lose time at work because of them.

Symptoms of dysphonia

▶ *Hoarseness*
▶ *Continual dry, sore throat*
▶ *Pain and discomfort when talking*
▶ *Sensation of continual drip at the back of the throat*
▶ *Heartburn*

- ▶ *Quavering voice*
- ▶ *Inability to project the voice*
- ▶ *Change in the sound of the voice*

Causes of dysphonia

The causes are multiple, but the most common ones include:

- ▶ *Laryngitis or inflammation of the voice box*
- ▶ *Infections of the upper respiratory tract*
- ▶ *Reflux of acid from the stomach – heartburn*
- ▶ *Nodules, polyps or tumours of the vocal cords*
- ▶ *Oedema or swelling of the larynx*
- ▶ *Voice strain*
- ▶ *Under-active thyroid gland*
- ▶ *Previous surgery on the neck with nerve damage to the vocal cords.*
- ▶ *Psychological causes from stress.*

If a voice problem persists for two weeks or more then you should see a GP. If the GP considers that an antibiotic is indicated then this should clear the problem within two weeks. If it persists, then a specialist referral to an Ear, Nose and Throat (ENT) surgeon is sensible, or even to a specialist Multi-Disciplinary Voice Clinic (MDVC), which is exclusively for voice problems. There an ENT surgeon and a speech therapist will assess and investigate the voice problem, often working with other disciplines like osteopathy, physiotherapy, singing advisors and psychologists.

A main part of the investigation consists of direct inspection of the larynx using specialized equipment to view the vocal cords and to record how they function.

Protect your voice

Here are a dozen tips for looking after your voice:

▶ *Keep yourself well hydrated – aim at drinking six to eight glasses of water a day.*
▶ *Avoid smoking. This is bad for your general health and it kills your voice.*
▶ *Learn how to project your voice properly.*
▶ *Always practise properly before a talking engagement.*
▶ *If you are a singer, have professional singing lessons.*
▶ *Practise talking, singing and humming. There is evidence that humming keeps the sinuses clear.*
▶ *Do not get into the habit of coughing to clear your throat. It jars the vocal cords and may contribute to vocal nodules formation.*
▶ *If you are going to be talking a lot then drink tap water, lemonade and warm drinks. It's best to avoid milk, which produces mucus, as well as cold drinks, which actually numb the throat and will make you more liable to strain the voice.*
▶ *After a lot of talking gargle with warm salt water or warm lemonade. Again, avoid iced drinks.*
▶ *Practise diaphragmatic breathing.*
▶ *Use a sound system if it is available.*
▶ *If you are talking for a long time use a saliva producer, a small sweet or mint in the corner of the mouth before you start talking. Get rid of it before you do talk since you do not want to risk choking. Also, it does not look good if you are chewing or moving something about in your mouth.*

VOICE PROJECTION

At the start of this chapter I described a few scenarios where people may run into trouble. This is most likely when they strive to project their voice to the far corners of a room or hall. If they are not used to doing it then it may come over as uncontrolled shouting, which at the end of the talk will almost certainly leave them feeling hoarse.

Top Tip

As a rule of thumb, if a room is larger than ten square metres you will have to project your voice above normal conversational pitch.

The secret of projection lies in the use of the vowels. Cast your mind back to Chapter 4 where we discussed the mechanism of speech. Vowels need voice! That means that you have to vibrate the vocal cords. The vowels are the volume producers –please remember that.

To get your voice volume up you need to focus your attention on the vowels as you speak. You will be surprised at how this lifts the voice and ultimately pitches it to the corners of the room. Just get a book, any book, and read it out loud as you would do normally. Then do it by emphasizing the vowels as you read. You will notice a difference. Try recording your voice as you do this.

The other thing that projects the voice is the flow of air over the vocal cords. See how long you can sustain a flow of air by counting numbers. Take a deep breath and then exhale, all the time counting 1-2-3-4-5-6-7..., and see how far you can go. You really want to be able to reach at least 20, but stop when you need to. You need air after all!

Now repeat this, but this time emphasize the vowels. Try recording the difference between the two. You will be surprised at the difference it makes.

To test how you are doing, and to give you a sense of how to project your voice, repeat all of these little exercises when you have a radio or a television playing in the background. In order to project you need to emphasize the vowels and increase the strength of that air flow. This means that you need to make sure that you are using good diaphragmatic breathing.

Use diaphragmatic breathing to project your voice. Look back at the little exercise I outlined in Chapter 1 to get you naturally breathing diaphragmatically. The deeper more efficient breathing will help you to throw your voice where it needs to go.

STRATEGY

AIM FOR CLARITY

There is a tendency as you project your voice to lose clarity with some words. Slowing the pace of your speech down will help. You can demonstrate this to yourself by again recording your voice as you read, then again as you project above a background noise such as the television. If you do this and emphasize the vowels then you will find yourself able to raise your voice level and project well.

Top Tip

Humming can actually lower your octave range and will help you to project your voice.

You will know if you are successfully projecting by the way that your throat feels. Successful voice projection will not produce any discomfort.

6

Small talk matters

Teas, where small talk dies in agonies.

Percy Bysshe Shelley (1792–1822)

A lot of people say they have no time for small talk or chit-chat. What they actually mean is that they are not very good at it and it fills them with dread. In truth, it need not and should not, if you arm yourself with strategies and aims. Indeed, once you have developed the art you will almost certainly enjoy it. Small talk is extremely important in establishing a rapport with someone in virtually all situations. Don't shy away from it, but make an effort to become adept at it.

Make time for pleasantries

Have you ever asked someone something and then received the curt reply, 'I've only got a minute.'

What they mean is they do not really want to talk or be engaged in conversation. You are unlikely to warm to the person. Yet if you handle the situation well, you may get them to warm to you, and if you talk well, you may persuade them that a minute is nowhere near long enough.

Perhaps, though, you quite often use that line on someone else? If you do, then it is likely that you also have a repertoire of lines such as 'I don't do small talk', 'I hate banal chat' and 'I haven't got time for gossip.' What you really mean is that you don't feel comfortable chatting. And if that is the case then you probably dislike other types of talking. You may cringe at the thought of public speaking, for example.

The first thing you need to do is lose the fear of small talk straight away. The next time you go into a shop, smile at the shop assistant, look them straight in the eye and say, 'Hello, how are you today?' And if they are wearing a name badge, use their name. Nine times out of ten you will be exchanging pleasantries without effort. You will have engaged them in conversation and you will have begun the process of teaching yourself how to talk to anyone.

This is a really easy way of starting off. People in shops are there waiting to serve you. Most people working in retail are 'people persons'. They usually like interacting with people and are likely to respond with a smile and to return simple pleasantries. You need not fear that you will run out of things to say, because the chances are that they will have other people to serve, other things to do, so any conversation will naturally be quite short.

But what you will find is that you will feel good for starting the conversation. You will have been the one to have broken the ice and you will actually have an advantage because you will know their name from their badge. Just watch their face, their eyes in particular, when you use their name. Everyone likes it when they are addressed in a friendly manner. If you are close enough you may see their pupils widen slightly. That is a great sign, which means that they are opening up to you.

Strategy

Make a point of looking at people's name badges in shops, banks, doctors' receptions and in offices. Use the names and do not feel embarrassed to do so.

Well, of course they don't. Yet, whenever you meet someone or are introduced, it is a good thing to try and commit that name to memory. Do not just shake hands, nod and then fumble for something to say. Make a conscious effect to remember the name and use it straight away in your first sentence. That way you will reinforce it in your memory.

If you did not catch the name, there is nothing wrong with stopping and saying, 'I am sorry, I did not quite catch your name.' Then when you are given it again you will see that the person is not irritated, but most often will register approval that you have clearly made an effort to remember their name. This is all about engagement.

If you find yourself in a conversation with someone and they have not offered their name, then offer yours. They will almost certainly reply by giving you their name, which you use straight away. And if they don't immediately give their name then ask them for it. Just ask 'And what is your name?'

Opening lines or opening gambits

You often hear people say that they start a conversation with their stock opening gambit. This may not be as good an idea as it seems. In some circumstances it can be a good move, but not in normal small talk. Let me explain.

A gambit is an opening move in the game of chess. The origin of the word is actually a contraction from the Italian phrase *dare il gambetto*, which is an encouragement to put your leg out to trip someone up. This was introduced to the game of chess in the mid-sixteenth century for an opening move designed to put the opponent off guard, possibly by making a sacrifice of a piece so that you gain an advantage.

A gambit is therefore a good move if you are entering a confrontational situation or you are about to engage in a debate or argument. It is not a good opener in small talk because your aim here is to engage and establish a rapport with another person, not win points. It is not to be regarded as a chess game to be won. Not unless you want to be regarded as arrogant or smug.

It is far better to regard your opener as an opening line rather than a gambit. It gets you into the correct psychological sphere.

Strategy

Be prepared. Commit some opening lines to memory. You might think that sounds banal, but it is common sense. The larger a stock of opening lines you have the better; otherwise you are only ever going to be able to start with a comment about the weather. That is often a good start, but it is not really scintillating, is it? And if the weather is miserable and dreary, how far do you propose to go with talking about that? It is simple logic that the larger your repertoire is then the more confident you will be and the better at small talk you will become.

So have a look at all these opening lines below. If you think that they look banal or somehow beneath you, then think again. They are neither banal nor beneath you. They are common openers used successfully every day to start conversations with neighbours, friends, colleagues, people waiting in queues and waiting rooms and so on. If you can get into the mindset of thinking of them for what they are – keys – then you will unlock the door that has for so long been such an obstacle to you.

Strategy

Get into the right mindset – determine to be sociable. Just tell yourself that instead of shying away from contact, conversations and communication at every available opportunity you are

going to become a sociable person. To do this aim to be the
initiator of a conversation at least three times a day.

WAITING IN A QUEUE

Try these opening lines:

'Don't you think waiting is fun?'
(You may be greeted with a surprised look, but it gives you an
opportunity to follow it up with a laugh, as if it was a joke. Or you
could explain that it simply gives you time to gather your thoughts,
plan something else, plot a novel, or whatever.)

'How do you feel when you are being kept waiting?'
(This could go in any direction. If you are being kept waiting
you may find that the other person is irritated or anxious or not
terribly bothered. Think about how it makes you feel. You may,
for example, be empathetic towards the person who is keeping
you waiting, since they may be under some strain. Or you may
be excited at the prospect of the activity or event that you are
queuing for.)

'Can you picture what would happen if the bus/train/plane etc. was
really late?'
(Here you are inviting the other person to extrapolate. You can
then follow it up by what it would mean to you and what you
would picture.)

'I love the sound of the train coming, don't you?'
(This opens up all sorts of possibilities for follow-ups. Why do
you like it? What sort of journey do you like best? What type of
transport do you like? What was your best journey?)

SITTING IN A WAITING ROOM

Here you have all sorts of things that you can talk about. Be careful about old favourites such as 'Do you come here often?' which may not sound right in a doctor's waiting room. Or 'What brings you here?' since that could be intrusive and unwelcome. Perhaps you could say something about the surroundings, the reading matter or the comfort of the seats.

'Do you think the seats are a bit regimented? Can you picture how much better it would be if they were scattered about?'
(Why would that be better? Would it relax people more?)

'Do you think that waiting rooms are designed to make you feel comfortable?'
(You can open up about different waiting rooms or areas, at airports, train stations, bus stations, comparing them with plush offices where you are being treated as a favoured guest rather than as a consumer.)

'Do you like the music in the background?'
(It could be intrusive. Is it appropriate for the type of waiting area you are in?)

'Do you like to see those sort of pictures or paintings on the wall?'
(You can broaden it to describe what the pictures mean to you and compare your opinion with what they mean to the other person.)

AT A DINNER TABLE

You may be with friends and have a readymade shared interest. Conversations can be started at virtually any point in that case since you have all gone past small talk exchanges. But if there are strangers that you are meeting for the first time, or other guests or if you are at a function with other delegates, then you may have to get in some conversation starters or ice breakers.

'Have you had a busy day?'
'What is a typical day for you?'
'How do you generally relax at the end of the day?'
'Where do you see yourself in another year?'
'What sort of music do you like to listen to?'
'Have you planned a holiday yet?'
'Have you seen any good movies recently?'
'Do you like reading?'
'What sort of books do you like best?'
'Do you play any sport?'
'What sports do you like to watch?'
'What do you like about watching...?'
'What do you think the next trend will be?'
'Can you see the best way for your company to develop?'
'How does an extra bank holiday sound to you?'
'That's a nice suit/dress/tie/shirt/necklace. What are your favourite colours?'
'Can you picture me in black/red/green?'
'How does a glass of red wine sound to you?'
'Do you use the computer much?'
'How would you feel if there was no Internet?'
'Can you imagine a world without mobile phones?'
'What are your feelings about social networking?'
'How do you think we can deal with the issue of childhood obesity?'
'Do you think that alcohol should be made more expensive?'
'What do you feel about people smoking outside restaurants?'

BUMPING INTO SOMEONE

This is the situation that many people with a social phobia hate, and they might spend their life taking evasive action to prevent chance encounters from occurring. But don't avoid it, change your thinking. Look forward to such happenings as opportunities to chat and forge friendships.

In this situation there are a whole series of questions that are begging to be asked:

> *'Oh I haven't seen you for ages. Tell me what you've been up to.'*
> *'Goodness, it has been a long time, hasn't it? Update me on the family.'*
> *'Lovely to see you. How is ... getting on?'*

And we could go on and on and on. There are lots of situations and the thing is that you can actually plan for them.

Strategy

Start planning for different situations. Get a little notebook and imagine meeting different people, both real and imaginary. And before you go to an event just consider whom you are going to meet, what sort of people are likely to be there, and what the opportunities to talk will be like.

Think up open questions to ask and write them down so that you have your own small talk prompt.

It might help to bunch the questions into the following groups:

▶ Location – *ask about the surroundings, where you are at that time.*
▶ Reason for being there – *both yours and the other person's. You can then volunteer why you are there, etc.*
▶ Future – *what you envisage happening later, as a result of the event, the occasion, etc. Where you will be in a month, in a year...whatever is appropriate.*

Appropriateness and crossing boundaries

Let us be clear. Your aim is to make yourself a better conversationalist, not a pest. The point about starting to chat to people is to show yourself that it is not difficult. It is not to give people the idea that you are trying to chat them up. That may be the case sometimes, but it depends upon whether or not you are in an appropriate situation or not. Waiting in a bus queue or a dental waiting room may not be the most appropriate place to try chatting up a member of the opposite sex, whereas a party or a bar may be.

Also be careful about boundaries. It is perfectly acceptable to chatter away with people but be sensitive and consider whether there are areas of conversation that should not be broached. Do not ask personal questions in small talk. You have to get to know someone before such questions will be welcome.

Adults must be wary of talking to children if they are unaccompanied by their parents or responsible adults. All children should have been told by their parents to be wary of talking to strangers and you should respect this. Indeed, some children take this message so much to heart that when they become adults they find that they do not like talking to people. You may even be such a person, but in reading this book you are taking steps to overcome any remaining reticence.

Don't delve into other people's relationships unless openings are made for you to do so.

Be careful about discussing age, appearance and body size. People may be very conscious about these matters. You do not want to come across as bullish and insensitive. Women may be sensitive about weight, whereas men may be sensitive about height and hair (or lack of it).

Building rapport with NLP

I have mentioned Neuro Linguistic Programming (NLP) earlier.
There are some very useful NLP techniques that will help you
in talking in general. Indeed, if you know about and absorb the
significance of the representational systems which we all use, you
can take a giant leap forwards in your ability to quickly build a
rapport with people.

First, a snapshot of NLP, a concept developed by Richard
Bandler and John Grinder in the 1970s. Their groundbreaking
book *Frogs into Princes* was a bestseller and began an extremely
useful therapeutic process that is widely used today. The aim
of NLP is to help the individual to learn and create good and
successful experiences, by looking at the way one thinks (neuro),
how one communicates (linguistic) and how you can teach
(programming) the mind to think, communicate and perform
more successfully.

In NLP there is a model of the way that we process
information. Essentially, we have all learned to structure our
experience through the use of the five senses – vision, hearing,
touch, smell and taste. You can think of these as being your
external senses because you sense the outer world with them.
But you also process information internally through *internal
senses* that twin with them. These are referred to as the
representational systems. There are three – visual, auditory
and kinaesthetic. Kinaesthetic refers to touch, or tactility,
but in NLP terms it also includes taste and touch. So the
representational systems are:

1 Visual – *when you picture, see or imagine.*
2 Auditory – *when you recollect or hear a conversation you had.*
3 Kinaesthetic – *when you feel or touch or experience.*

We all use all three of these inner senses at times, but most people have a dominant one that is their main way of thinking. You will be able to pick it up quite quickly when you start listening to people. They will tend to use words and language appropriate to the way that they are thinking.

Before you do anything, your mind formulates a thought and it is apparent to you as a visual, auditory or kinaesthetic experience. When you talk, the words that you choose will tend to reflect that inner representation. And this gives you a clue as to how the brain or the mind sorts your experiences.

This may be a new concept to you but give it some time to mature. Observe and listen to people and you will begin to see how they are expressing the way that they think. If you can pick up on that and then deliberately use the same pattern of expression back at them in your small talk then you will begin to build a rapport straight away.

Typical words used include:

▶ Visual: *see, visualize, picture, imagine, show, view*
▶ Auditory: *hear, listen, sound, talk, resonate, echo, call out*
▶ Kinaesthetic: *feel, touch, weight it up, toss it about, walk, throw about.*

Now flick back a few pages and go through some of the opening lines that were suggested. You may not have noticed first time round, but you will realize now that some were designed for visual, some for auditory and others for kinaesthetic ways of thinking/talking. You will not know, of course, about a person's representational system straight away, unless you have already observed and listened to the cues that they give in their speech, but having a selection of different types of openers will give you the opportunity to find out.

Some people are innately good at this. A good salesperson will probably tune in and pitch their language at a customer. In a sense they are conversational chameleons, altering the way that they communicate to resonate with their client. It is not a gimmick; it is a very powerful and quite legitimate method of communication.

On the other hand, some people are not good at picking up on this at all and they blunder around, never really getting to know their fellows. People can be in a lifelong relationship yet never truly understand that their partner thinks in a different manner. One may be a visual and the other an auditory or a kinaesthetic. The gifts that they give one another may reflect their own representational system, so may never quite resonate in the same way as they would if had they been 'appropriate'. A visual likes things they can see – they like colours, pictures, books. Auditories like music, things they can hear. And kinaesthetics like tactility, things they can feel and which they can feel something about.

Strategy

Begin straight away to observe and listen to everyone's conversation and the content of their speech. Note the representational words they use and deliberately start formulating your speech to be in accord with theirs.

Openers should be open

Opening lines should be as open-ended as possible. That is, you really want to try to avoid closed questions that can be answered with a simple yes or no, or which will be followed by a few words so that the conversation quickly peters out. If you ask open-ended questions that permit the other conversant to expand and volunteer information then it should be a simple matter of keeping the conversation going. You will find that in small talk people tend to adopt an unwritten format whereby one person talks, then pauses long enough to allow the other person to speak, and so on alternately. Rather like table tennis.

Some people are so fond of their own voices that they will try to dominate a conversation. It is up to you, of course, how you respond. Do you let them go on bullishly talking, or do you interrupt and make your contribution? The good thing is that these people are liable to respond very well to open-ended questions.

If you look at the openers that have been given you will see that most are questions that suggest that you want more information than a yes or no. They are invitations to communicate and expand. That is an open question and it should be your aim to keep lobbing them up.

Now you are talking

The initial exchanges are over and then comes the middle part of the process, the art of keeping the conversation flowing. Your aim is to prevent awkward gaps and pauses that make it seem as if the conversation is a struggle. If there are only two people then this can be extremely awkward. If there are more than two, then there is ample opportunity to direct an open-ended question at someone else.

You may have found a thread from the initial exchange of questions and answers, which means that you are off and away. If not, then you can now safely start a new thread. Once again, if you have a strategy then you can easily get started. You may find it easy to use the acronym FILM. This stands for family, interests, living and miscellaneous questions:

- Family – *ask what family the person has, then follow any thread that looks or sounds promising.*
- Interests – *what are the other person's interests? Hobbies, politics, sport, holidays. It will open up a myriad of possibilities.*
- Living – *what do they do for a living? If not working, how do they spend their time etc?*
- Miscellaneous – *here you build up a series of questions, about current books, movies, political situation, or you can ask what they think about social situations, art or science. Literally anything goes.*

This still all amounts to small talk. If you are at a business event or a social occasion, then you can naturally lead into a topic to do with that. And whatever it is, because you will have been thinking of the other person's inner representational system, you should have built up a rapport that will carry this part of the conversation through successfully.

Closing down

This should not be difficult. Either of you can do it. The aim is affability and the desire to leave the conversation as though you have had a pleasant and interesting time:

'Goodness, the time has flown. And so must I.'
'That has been so interesting.'
'I would love to stay and chat more, but I have to get to...'

Whether you drop an invitation to meet again is up to you. It can either be a firm one or a loose one, or even just a suggestion that perhaps you ought to do it again. Or even a simple 'I hope we bump into each other again.'

To summarize...

Think of small talk as having three components – opening, maintenance and close-down:

1 Opening

Be prepared for every situation. Begin a notebook and think of opening questions that you can use for all sorts of situations – in queues, waiting rooms, bumping into people, parties, business events.

Bunch your questions about location, reason for being there, the future from that point.

Try to pick up the other person's representational system – are they a visual, auditory or kinaesthetic. Use the appropriate language and communication to build a rapport.

2 Maintenance

Follow threads that are offered. If needs be change direction and start a new thread by asking about FILM – family, interests, living and miscellaneous.

3 Close-down

Aim to leave the impression that you have enjoyed the chat, have been interested and that you have bonded with the other person or persons.

Now go and start enjoying small talk!

7

How you look, act and say

Action is eloquence.

William Shakespeare

Consider the title of this chapter for a moment. What does it mean to you? I mean, apart from being a little wordplay on 'work, rest and play'.

The book is about talking, so just consider yourself in a talking situation. Which of these three things matters most to you? Is it the way you look? The way you act or behave? Or is it the way that you say things?

We are basically talking about the NLP representational system again, of course, so your answer may well reflect what is the most important aspect in terms of your own preferred system. If you are a visual you probably want to look good, a kinaesthetic will relate to the way you behave, and an auditory will probably focus in on the sound.

If you have a worry about talking, perhaps a worry about making a speech or making a presentation in front of a class or an audience of some sort, where does the actual content come into the equation?

Think back to a speech you heard, a lesson given by a teacher, a lecture by one of your lecturers or a presentation at a conference. What was it about and how much do you remember of it? Do you remember the whole of it or just an impression? The chances are that you only took in a proportion of it, a few points. Yet you gave it an unconscious assessment. It would have been good, medium or indifferent.

Top Tip

A good presentation or lecture is all about performance.

In terms of that performance the 7%–38%–55% rule gives you an idea of what makes the most impact with people:

Body language – 55 per cent

Tone and how you sound – 38 per cent

Content – 7 per cent

In the context of all verbal communications this can only be regarded as rule of thumb. See below for more about the 7%–38%–55% rule.

The point is that you need to lose the idea that when you talk you have to be word perfect and content perfect. Your aim should be to appear confident. If you can do that, then people will be impressed.

The eyes say a lot

Let us go back a step, because I want to build on the concept of the representational systems (see Chapter 6) and how you can assess which one people tend to use. It is worth getting a good grip on this, because it will help you to assess the messages they are giving you, which in turn will help you to mirror it back at them. This will all help in the building of a rapport.

Grinder and Bandler referred to all of this in their book *Frogs into Princes*. They felt that the sense-related language people use is linked to certain eye movements that they unconsciously make. You will almost certainly be aware that by and large people do not look directly at you all the time that they are speaking. Their eyes flicker about. Indeed, some people never make eye contact, but seem to be looking all over the area around you, or keep looking in one particular direction. That in itself may be telling you quite a lot.

Grinder and Bandler described the most common eye movements as shown in Figure 7.1.

Upward movements tend to be visual; sideways auditory; and downwards to the right (for a right-handed individual)

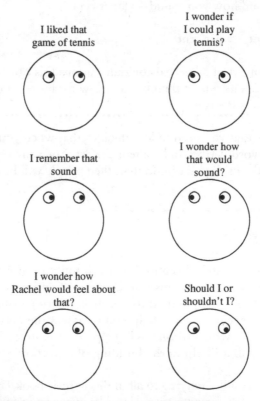

Figure 7.1 Eye movements give you clues about what someone is thinking.

kinaesthetic, when grasping a concept or feeling it. Downwards to the left was thought to be auditory, when having an inner dialogue, or talking it over in the mind.

Looking upward to the right tends to be when you're recollecting a memory of how something looks visually. Looking upwards to the left occurs when imagining or constructing how something would look visually.

Similarly, looking sideways to the right would represent remembering a sound, while looking sideways to the left would be imagining how something would sound.

You can try this out simply by observing and listening to people as they talk. People are often very surprised to find that the eye movements are often accompanied by the appropriate sensory language.

And once again, using that same type of language can help you to build that rapport:

Visual

'I can see your point.'
'I can see what you mean.'
'Can you just picture that?'
'I wonder if you can visualize…'
'It is just so colourful.'
'And he used such colourful language'.

Auditory

'That sounds good to me.'
'I hear what you are saying.'
'It is just what I was talking about.'
'That is music to my ears.'
'No one listens any more.'

Kinaesthetic

'I felt that it was right.'
'You have touched upon it.'
'I was just numbed by it.'
'It pulls at your heartstrings.'
'I thought it smelled fishy.'

STRATEGY

Strategy

Just informally observe people as you chat. See if you can detect their eye movement and listen to the sensory words they use. Try using the same sensory language as they do.

AND YOU SHOULD USE YOUR EYES AS WELL

By this I do not mean that you should actively aim at making eye movements. Rather I mean that you should cultivate the habit of giving people your full attention. Look them in the eye, make eye contact and become aware of the muscles around your face.

Making eye contact is one of the most important things you can do in conversations with people, whether that is when chatting with one person, as a member of a group, or even when speaking in front of a large audience. When people see you looking at them, not darting your glance away quickly, then you will connect with them. And that is always a prime aim when talking.

Notice also the state of dilation of the other person's pupils, assuming that you can see well enough and you are close enough to do so. Dilation of the pupil is generally a good sign because the person is opening up to you, and they are warming to you.

Top Tip
If you can see the little dolls in someone's eyes you know they are opening up to you.

The word 'pupil' comes from the Latin *pupilla*, meaning 'little doll'. The more dilated the pupils the bigger you will see your reflection in them, like a little doll in each eye.

The 3-Vs – verbal, vocal and visual content

Consider that little rule of thumb, the 7%–38%–55% rule that I mentioned earlier. Do you find it surprising that how you look and act has far more importance in terms of the impact you make than the content of your message?

Of course you are surprised. It probably flies in the face of all of your ideas about talking. The good news is that because of this you have plenty of scope for improving the way that you perform when you talk, whether that is in a simple conversation with one person or when you deliver a speech, lecture or give a presentation.

I emphasize that this is a rule of thumb because it is something that seems to apply to most speaking situations. If you look at any documentary you will see this. You are more likely to warm to someone who has a good presentational style, who looks squarely at the camera and talks in an appropriate tone. You see this especially with politicians. Some seem so gifted that you can watch, listen and be persuaded about their policies, even although they actually hold views that are diametrically opposed to your own. On the other hand, others who are less adept may not be so persuasive, despite holding the same values as you.

Albert Mehrabian is Emeritus Professor of Psychology at UCLA in America. He has conducted research into communication and body language over a 40-year period. In 1971 he formulated two general conclusions about face-to-face communication. Firstly, that there are three elements involved – words, tone of voice and non-verbal behaviour. (By non-verbal behaviour he specifically meant facial expressions.) Secondly, that these elements contribute to the feelings and attitudes that will be communicated in the proportion of 7% words, 38% tone and 55% body language. This has been widely circulated in communication seminars around the world as the 7%–38%–55% rule. It is sometimes also referred to as the 3-Vs rule – verbal, vocal and visual.

As a respected academic Professor Mehrabian has been concerned about the way that his work has been applied as a general rule to all communication, when in fact he states that it only has relevance when one is considering how someone will like the person who is delivering the message. He did not mean it to imply that the majority of the message itself was delivered by non-verbal means. It is the impact or empathy that is engendered.

I have no wish to add to this confusion, which is why I have emphasized that in general communication this can only be used as a rule of thumb, because it does generally seem to have validity in terms of how well people will empathize with you when you talk. It is not categorical, but it is a useful guideline.

Body language

Body language is so important. You say a lot to someone in this manner. This is very important if you want to impress and communicate well, whether one to one, to a group or to the media.

Top Tip
The majority of people go on first impressions. They form an impression within the first few seconds, strongly based on body language and the way someone acts. You probably do as well.

The ancient Greeks and the Romans were interested in aspects of body language as they appertained to talking. In Greece people practised the arts of rhetoric, oratory and sophistry. They loved to debate, act and argue, so talking skills were ranked highly. Accordingly, different schools of philosophy arose and people paid professional sophists to teach them how to talk and win arguments. We shall return to this in Chapter 12 on 'Winning arguments'.

Marcus Tullius Cicero (106–43 BC) was a Roman orator, writer, lawyer, politician and statesman. Among his many works he wrote *Rhetorica* (Writings on Rhetoric) and *Orationes* (Orations), in which he discussed the importance of gestures to indicate and emphasize feelings and points the orator means to make.

Sir Francis Bacon (1561–1626), philosopher, statesman, writer and scientist, was interested in all areas of human endeavour and wrote about the way that acting can enhance the ability to communicate:

> *It is a thing indeed (acting), if practisd professionally, of low repute, but if it be made a part of discipline, it is of excellent use. I mean stage playing, an art which strengthens the memory, regulates the tone and effect of the voice and pronunciation, teaches a decent carriage of the countenance and gesture, gives not a little assurance, and accustoms young men to bear being looked at.*

If you disregard the disparaging Elizabethan attitude towards the profession of acting, you will see that this is excellent advice highly relevant to the subject of this chapter.

Charles Darwin (1809–82), the great naturalist who made the single greatest scientific breakthrough in 1859 when he published his theory of evolution in his book *Origin of Species,* was interested in all aspects of communication and behaviour. One of his later works, *The Expression of the Emotions in Man and Animals* (1872), focused people's attention on body language. This laid the foundation for the science of 'ethology', the study of behaviour and body language.

In 1967 Desmond Morris wrote a popular book, *The Naked Ape*, which brought body language and human behaviour into the public mind. He followed this up with a series of other books, notably *Manwatching* in 1977.

Nowadays ethology is literally big business, since most companies understand that to attract business you have to have effective communication, good marketing and most importantly people who can go out and present their company in a positive light. They send people on courses to learn how to talk, perform and project in order to communicate in the business world.

Body language encompasses the way that you move, your gestures, facial expressions, mannerisms and even body tics. It also includes the way that you hold yourself, stand, sit or lie in the presence of other people. More than that, it includes your personal space; how much of a gap you allow between yourself and others, and the way that you touch or fiddle with objects, or the way that you hold a drink, smoke a cigarette, or hold a glass. And very importantly, it includes your general tactility with other people.

That means that it covers a lot of ground. There may be a lot that you are already doing that is sending out good signals. It is also possible that there is a lot that you are doing which is giving the wrong messages or sending out signals that you are either not aware of or do not intend to do so. If all of that is happening in the first few seconds you meet someone, you may be making quite the wrong first impression.

'MIRROR, MIRROR ON THE WALL'

You should use a mirror to study yourself. Indeed, if you are going to give a presentation or speech then a mirror is one of the best tools you can use in your preparation. Mirrors are great things because they reflect back your image and they show you what other people see. To get the best out of your mirror you have to be prepared to use it in two ways – firstly, as a tool so that you can observe how you look and act, and, secondly, as a tool to help you rectify problems and practise how to perform.

Top Tip

You can practise using body language to emphasize what you want to say.

I want you to note that I used the word 'perform'. You probably never think of your talking as performing, but that is just what it is. You are performing in front of one or more people, and your intention is to impart some idea, some emotion or some information. Whether that is a first date, an attempt to impress your partner's parents, business colleagues or an auditorium full of people, it is a performance. Shed the idea that there is anything wrong with that. Don't worry if it sounds as if you are not being natural, or that you are not being true to yourself. All interactions are performances. The more you perform them the more natural they will seem. The important thing is to start to cut out the things that do not enhance your performance and start to incorporate the things that do.

Strategy: First reflections

Take any situation where you are going to be talking, whether that is a conversation with an aunt, a consultation with your doctor or a presentation that you have to give. Go into a room on your own, one with a full-length mirror and have that talk. Just do it to the mirror, as if the mirror is the person or persons that you are going to be talking to. Improvise or give your presentation and keep doing it for three minutes. Don't rehearse, backtrack or stop and start again. Just go through it and keep talking, all the while looking at how you are performing.

At the end of the three minutes, or more if you are in full flow, stop and reflect on how well you did.

Did you notice any odd mannerisms? Did you stutter, stumble or repeat one expression or another? Did you fidget, fiddle with hands, your spectacles, a pen or some article of clothing?

Did you appear confident? Was your body language appropriate, or were you waving your hands around needlessly, emphasizing things aimlessly? Did you stand confidently or were you dashing about like a cat on a hot tin roof?

Be honest with yourself. Was it a good performance?

WHAT TO LOOK FOR

I expect that you did not feel very happy with that performance. It did not seem as crisp as you would like it to be. Apart from that you are not really sure why. It may have seemed to lack confidence or polish, or you seemed a bit nervous, even though it was just yourself that you were performing for.

I want you to disregard the things that you said and instead focus on three things. Your face and facial expressions, your posture, and your gestures and mannerisms.

Face and expressions
Did you focus on your face? Of course you did. It is the main thing that people do in close situations. You were in a close enough situation as you looked into that full-length mirror.

Would it surprise you to know that there are basically only six basic facial expressions? Charles Darwin wrote about these in his book *The Expressions of the Emotions in Man and Animals* in 1872. It makes fascinating reading for it reveals the painstaking way that Darwin went about collecting his data and material. He had no cine-cameras, no videos, no way of recording moving images. He did it by painstaking research and by sending detailed questionnaires to fellow naturalists in order to accumulate a substantial amount of information from various observers.

He concluded that these six basic facial expressions are common to all humans regardless of their race or place of origin. They are essentially inherited.

They are the emotions of happiness, sadness, fear, surprise, anger and disgust.

Now, before you go any further, stop reading, go to a mirror and run through all of those six expressions. Go through them all, and just get the impression. Then come back to the book and bring a mirror with you or sit by your mirror.

Strategy: Practise the six basic expressions

Practise the basic six expressions in the mirror. It does not matter how pantomimic they seem; the point is you can do all of them quite naturally. Do this every morning as you wash or after you have brushed your teeth. Practising muscle movements will allow you to develop your range of facial expression.

Darwin set about trying to analyse these expressions by focusing on which parts of the face were involved in making expressions. He looked at whether the expression was made by the eyes, the eyebrows, the mouth or combination movements of several parts of the face.

What did you find? Were you aware of whether you moved muscles around your eyes when you made a happy expression, or did you just use your mouth? When you showed surprise did you just open your eyes wide, or did the eyebrows rise and the jaw drop open? When you looked sad did the eyebrows move the same way as they did when you were surprised?

The fact is that the muscles of facial expression have great ability to move the face into all sorts of positions to convey whatever emotions you want. By and large you do it naturally, as in the six basic expressions, but you modify them according to your personality and how much of yourself that you want to show people.

Now with the mirror in front of you once again go through the gamut of expressions, but this time look at what parts of the face you move to form the expression.

Anatomically, the facial muscles are disposed around the orifices of the eyes, nose, mouth and ears as sphincters and dilators. A sphincter is essentially a ring of muscle in the body that has the purpose of opening or closing an opening. A dilator is a muscle that pulls on a sphincter to help open it up.

The large sphincter muscle around the mouth forms the lips and has the function of closing the mouth. It is called the *orbicularis oris*. When you contract it you will pucker the lips. The sphincter muscles around the eyes are called the *orbicularis oculi*, and their purpose is to narrow the eyes and close them.

You will also notice that some muscles which pull the mouth up into a smile have attachments that affect the eyes and the nose. See also how the large *frontalis muscle*, the main forehead muscle elevates the brow and yet others will alter the angulation of the eyebrows and of the mouth.

The point I want you to absorb is that everyone has broadly speaking the same set of facial muscles. We have the same basic expressions. Yet some people are more expressive than others. That is simply because they have *allowed* themselves to be expressive. You can too, which is what I want you to start practising.

Look in the mirror and try to make the various muscles that I have outlined above, work on your own face. Experiment, get to know your face and its potential. See if you can modify the various expressions.

The single most important facial expression I want you to practise is smiling. This is the expressive sign that shows that you are happy.

Strategy: Smile!

Whenever you meet someone from now on, smile. Don't wait for them to smile first before you tentatively reciprocate. Make it part of your personality.

Go back to your mirror, imagine a number of different scenarios and smile at the mirror as if it was a person. If your natural smile pleases you that is great. Just look to see whether you are smiling with your whole face, the eyes as well as the mouth. Obviously you will find that some smiles are more suitable on some occasions than others. In general, people warm to a smiling face.

Practise your smile to show that you are happy...

▶ *to be somewhere*
▶ *to meet somebody*
▶ *to receive something*
▶ *for someone*
▶ *to have been invited*
▶ *to be able to pass on good news*
▶ *because life is good.*

This really is a splendid exercise. A smile at the start of a conversation is a great ice-breaker. The more you practise it the more natural all of the smiles become. Add this exercise to your six expressions exercise when you wash.

Finally, practise making eye contact. Do it in the mirror. It is easy, just look deeply into your own eyes. Get to know that face of yours intimately. See how comfortable it is to look directly into your own eyes. That is what you should aim at with other people. Ensure that you look right into their pupils. It will show that you are giving them your entire attention. Remember, you are looking to see the little doll in their pupils.

Signs of anxiety

All of the following physical actions or phenomena may betray the fact that you are feeling anxious. They are things that you want to avoid if you can. Some are easier to overcome than others. The physiological ones will all tend to disappear as you put the various strategies that are mentioned in Chapter 1 into action. The others are all to do with how you act and behave, which come under the next two headings about body posture and mannerisms.

▶ *Over-breathing*
▶ *Shaking*
▶ *Sweating*
▶ *Continually drying your hands*
▶ *Blushing*
▶ *Quavering voice*
▶ *Nervous coughing*
▶ *Obvious swallowing*
▶ *Lack of eye contact*
▶ *Fidgeting with hands*
▶ *Fidgeting with hair*
▶ *Fidgeting with clothes*
▶ *Fidgeting with jewellery, cufflinks or rings*
▶ *Pacing*
▶ *Shifting posture*
▶ *Inappropriate gestures*
▶ *Folding arms and closed position*

Body posture
This is very important. If you have ever watched a lecture or listened to a speech where the speaker clearly wanted to be

elsewhere, then you will understand what I mean. When someone is squirming and hating being in the limelight then you can generally tell. Their body language proclaims it to all and sundry, which is exactly what they do not want to do.

Here is the best news possible. It does not have to be this way. All you have to do is be aware of your own body movements and control the body language. Instantly, people will take you as being confidant rather than the tongue-tied person you previously thought of yourself as being.

Strategy: looking confident

Use your mirror to practise looking confident. If you act confidently (even when you are not feeling confident) then that is how people will remember you and react to you.

I will be looking at this throughout the book, since different situations may require different attention to the posture. In general whether you are standing or sitting you need to look both natural and confident.

If you are giving a lecture or a speech one of the most obvious signs of nervousness is if you dash about the platform or stage, unable to stand still. You should aim to face the audience, allowing your hands and arms to hang naturally so that you are standing neither with your hands held in front of you nor clasped behind your back. The former tends to be a defensive, nervous posture and the latter can seem wooden, as if you are about to give out a carefully rehearsed poetry recitation.

You can move, of course, but make the movements appropriate. Walk to another part of the dais or platform to address another segment of the audience. And if you do that, use your eyes to hold their regard, to show that you are interested in them.

If you are in a sitting situation, then sit properly in the chair. Don't slouch, sprawl, balance of the edge or rock back on the legs. Sit comfortably, properly and engage with your fellows. Be able to turn to other parties present, but do so naturally.

If you are in a standing and chatting situation then again you need to give a confident pose. Don't be hopping from one foot to another, bobbing up and down on your feet or swaying back and forth or rocking from side to side. All of them imply discomfort and possible nervousness. In these situations use your eyes, use your facial expression and use appropriate gestures.

Mannerisms and gestures

The way that you use your limbs can have a huge impact on how well you perform. Many people just cannot keep their hands off their heads and faces when they are in talking situations. This is one of the things that I would counsel you against. If you are giving a talk in front of people then consider that your face is out of bounds. If you are forever scratching your nose, covering your mouth with your fingers, tugging at ears, then your audience will register each gesture. It does not look pleasant and it does not look confident.

How often do you see confident characters in movies covering the lower part of their face with their hand? You may do this naturally if you are thinking, but do not do it when talking. Certainly not if you want to appear confident.

Fidgeting with hands, jewellery or pens does become irritating for people to watch. You do not need to do it, so don't. Aim at making any gestures natural and appropriate.

I will be covering the topic quite specifically when I come to discuss presentations, lectures and speeches later in the book, but for now just take this one thing on board. Try to keep your hands apart. Don't fold them together or hold them. All of those are defensive moves that suggest that you are not fully comfortable. Instead, aim at keeping them naturally at your side, or allow them to rest on the arms of the chair.

Avoid also unnecessary extravagant hand gestures if you are explaining things. As soon as you start moving your hands people will automatically follow the hand movements. If you watch any discussion programme, especially with politicians, you will see a range of interesting gestures, not many of which actually make sense. Some people use a karate chopping gesture to emphasize points, others jab fingers, still other clench their fists and make hammering moves to illustrate their points. The thing is that these gestures usually mean little to anyone except themselves. If you watch people and analyse their gestures you will see what I mean.

One of the best things you can do is to allow your palms to be seen from time to time. This is almost universally taken to be an open and honest gesture. It is very useful when presenting.

Avoid crossing your arms over your chest. Everyone knows that it is usually an insecure and defensive gesture. The same goes for your legs. When you cross both together, then you are sending out a message that you are not comfortable in the situation. This may surprise you, because you may do this when you are relaxing at home. Yet for most people it implies that you would rather be at home than with them.

Top Tip

Appropriate body language can be used very persuasively. We shall look at this in the section on presentations

How you say things

From the 7%–38%–55% rule of thumb, we know how you say things can have a huge, 38% impact on how people relate to you.

Obviously if you are a mumbler then people will have to strain to listen to you. If you are a grumbler, they will soon get fed up with your moaning tone. And if you are a bumbler, they will think of you as exactly that – someone who bumbles along and who cannot be taken seriously.

The way that you say things and the tone that you use need practice just as much as the way you look and behave.

The first thing that you must not do if you find yourself in a situation where you have to speak out in public is to apologize. Never apologize for being yourself. If you stand and announce that you are not very good at talking, or that you do not think you can tell people very much, then you will have given them a message before you even deliver any of the information that you want to impart. They will already have started to switch off.

Even if you do not feel comfortable, never admit it. Get up and pretend to be confident. It's as simple as that. You get up and act the part of a confident person. And that includes making your voice, your tone, seem confident. You do not actually have to be as eloquent as Sir Winston Churchill or Professor Brian Cox, the particle physicist, but if you aim to talk with as few ums and ahs as you can, then you will come across as being confident.

Once again your mirror is your great friend. Talking should be practised. Talk into the mirror; practise your speech, your conversation, your presentation. Talk to your dog, your cat, your family and your friends.

The tone of your voice is worth practising. Don't try to be someone else, but do try to develop your own voice. Recording yourself on a video or on a mobile phone will give you an idea of how you sound. You should be aware, however, that most people do not sound the same in all situations. When you are with friends or relatives you are likely to be at your most natural. When you are speaking to people you know less well the voice may tend to become a bit higher. And when you are completely out of your comfort zone the voice may start to quaver a little. You may even find that you have a slight stutter. If you find this happens then look again at Chapter 4 on 'Hesitation and stammering'.

TONE-MATCHING

If you are aiming to build a rapport with someone then tone-matching is worth doing.

People can vary their voice through its:

▶ *volume*
▶ *tempo or speed*
▶ *tone*
▶ *pitch.*

Just think about how alteration of any or all of these can impart meaning to a voice. If you watch a film in a foreign language that you cannot translate, you will know how much information will be conveyed to you through the ways that the actors use their voices. Anger, jealousy, depression, you think of it, alterations of the above factors can convey the appropriate emotion.

Rapport with someone is built by matching their tone and the rest of these factors.

Strategy

Listen to conversations about you and note how people alter the four factors of volume, tone, pitch and speed of voice in different types of conversation.

Then when you are next in conversation with a stranger try to empathize by tone-matching.

Practice makes perfect (or almost)

Although talking is a natural activity, it does need practice. Like any other activity the more practice you do the more adept you will become until you reach a stage of proficiency. Having said that, it can be a little like playing golf, whereby you practise the swing that you use to strike the ball. Anyone can improve their swing to a certain level, but if your technique is flawed, then you will reach a point where you are simply practising how to repeat the flaws.

In the chapters that follow we will look at all sorts of strategies that you can put into practice in order to ensure that from now on you are only practising the good speech habits.

8

Dinner parties

All parties are meant to be fun. Dinner parties are essentially social affairs centred around a meal. The type of meal can vary immensely and so too can the type of talking that is involved:

▶ 'Come for a meal' – *When you receive this sort of invitation it usually implies that it will be a casual occasion where you are expected to fit in with the normal eating arrangements of the host. As such you probably simply need to be smart casual. The topics of conversation are likely to be light and not too taxing.*

▶ 'Come to our dinner party' – *This is more likely to be a structured meal with other guests. You will be expected to integrate and contribute.*

▶ 'We are throwing a dinner party and would like you to come' – *You may feel that you are making up the numbers. Do not let this colour your enjoyment. It is not as if you will find yourself stuck in a corner with no one to talk to.*

▶ 'We are having some friends round to dinner and want you to come.' – *This is different; you are one of the friends. The purpose of the meal is established and you can go feeling valued.*

▶ 'Come for dinner, there is someone interesting I want you to meet.' – *This is a set-up for some reason. Perhaps the host wants to introduce you to a prospective romantic partner, someone with a shared interest or a business opportunity. There is no harm in asking, since you do not want any sudden surprises. Or do you?*

▶ 'You are invited to a formal dinner' – *This sounds like a black tie and formal dress affair at a sit-down dinner. You will probably have to be on good behaviour. Not a time to crack ribald jokes.*

▶ 'We would like you to speak at the annual dinner party' – *This does sound serious. You are actually being asked to perform a part. It may be the after-dinner speech to a club or society, or it could be a group that you yourself belong to. In a sense you are the guest of honour, so you must behave as such. You will need to be in character throughout the affair and be able to get up, in the correct character and manner, and deliver whatever type of speech you are expected to make.*

▶ 'Come for a family meal' – *If it is your own family, then all is well. Time to catch up and enjoy re-establishing bonds. Or it could be a meal to meet your boyfriend's or girlfriend's family. A time to be on good behaviour.*

Preparing for the dinner party

The point is that the type of dinner party it is will affect both the part you play in the proceedings and how much attention you can expect to be focused on you. You can prepare accordingly.

You might think that the host (and I shall use the word host for host or hostess) has all the preparing to do. That is not the case. If you want to enjoy the event, then an event is how you should regard it. Approach it as something a little out of the ordinary, as a special occasion and you will get more out of it. Sharing food is, after all, one of the most profound and basic things that human beings can do. When you are invited to partake of food that someone else has prepared you should feel honoured that for that event they are sharing part of their life with you.

You may think that sounds grander than it actually will be. If you do regard it in those terms, however, then you will come across as enthusiastic, friendly and good company. You will play your part in making the event a success.

FIND OUT WHO WILL BE THERE

Do not think it is rude to ask. It shows that you are eager and interested. Your host may not wish to disclose the guest list to you, in which case there may be conclusions that you can draw. Either the guest list has not been confirmed and others may be asked, or you are being kept in the dark because there is someone special that they want you to meet. In that case you know that there may be an agenda that is being kept from you and you can prepare yourself.

FIND OUT A LITTLE ABOUT THEM

Once again this is not rude; it shows interest. Simply ask your host. You do not have to ask for a detailed history on everyone, just a thumbnail description of their interests and background.

If you know of someone else who is invited, then they may know about the other guests. You can subtly ask for information in a polite manner. Phrase it in such a way that it shows that you are looking forward to meeting the other guests.

All information that you have will allow you to find out a few facts about their interests so that you can add them to your repertoire of opening questions or 'change of subject' tacks. Have a look back at Chapter 6 on 'Small talk matters' and see how you can fit such questions and change of tacks together.

If a guest is a writer, find out what sort of things they write. Look up a few reviews on the Internet. If they play golf or any other sport, find out a little about the rules and which professional player or team is doing well at the moment. If they keep tropical fish, grow orchids, go scuba diving, bungee jumping or like to travel, find out a few general things on those subjects.

You may discover that they have an interesting occupation or that they have performed some fascinating or important role in society; make it your business to find out about it. There will probably be information on the Internet that will help you.

KNOW WHAT IS HAPPENING IN THE WORLD

You may not be a regular newspaper reader, but before you go to your dinner party make sure that you are aware of current news. Check out the newspapers, the news on television or on the Internet.

Who the guests are may help you to focus on which areas of the news you should know about. It is always a good idea to know about the current headlines. There will be something that is contentious and which will be a potential area for discussion. If you are the person who introduces it then you are in control at that point. People will focus on you.

Find out about the latest main sporting headlines. That goes down well at most dinner parties. You just need to know enough to facilitate a conversation and it shows that you have taken an interest.

Be careful about conversation-stoppers. Those are highly contentious topics that people may have strong views about. Stepping on someone's beliefs is one common type of conversation-stopper. Someone may be a devout believer in some religion and will not take kindly to someone declaring that atheism is the only logical conclusion for a thinking person.

One or more people may be embarrassed about a conversation-stopping remark, so take care in introducing something that causes people to pull up their personal drawbridge. The person who uttered such a faux pas will be remembered and there may be lingering tension throughout the meal. The other thing of course is that such a topic can have the effect of inciting an argument, so just be prepared to fight your corner if need be. Remember, also, that if you are a guest, then an argument may not be something that your host was expecting you to start.

Strategy

Be prepared by finding out a little about your fellow guests and their interests.

Your role as a guest

That is correct, you do have a role. It is not just to go, eat, drink, laugh and go away at the end of the meal. You are expected to participate in some way.

RICE – THE GUEST'S ROLE MNEMONIC

Keep these in mind and you will fulfil the role of a good guest at a dinner party:

R is for Respectfulness – you are a guest. Be respectful of your host and your fellow guests.

I is for Interest – your preparation should help to show that you are interested in each person present and that you find their views interesting.

C is for chatty – you are not expected to sit and eat without contributing to the conversation, so you should try to be chatty. You do not have to take over the conversation, but you should contribute to it and help to keep it going.

E is for etiquette – you should aim to be polite and show good manners. It also stands for entertained, which is what your host hopes everyone will be. And it also stands for enlightened, which is what should happen afterwards, you will go away having learned something about your host and fellow guests. And it possibly also stands for enlisted, if you have used the dinner party to network.

HOST – THE HOST'S ROLE MNEMONIC

This is an easy one to remember:

H is for Hospitality – of course. Enough said.

O is for Observation – you need to see all that is happening, never ignore a guest and spot any problems. It is not just about keeping glasses filled.

S is for Solicitousness – you need to be ready to look after all of your guests.

T is for Toleration – you are there to cater for and attend to your guests, not to argue with them or make them feel uncomfortable. You have to tolerate their behaviour – unless it oversteps the bounds of common courtesy, of course.

Strategy

Remember RICE for the guest's role and HOST for the host's role.

Dinner party etiquette

The dinner party doesn't just start with the meal, of course. It is the central part of the event, but there are important bits before and after you sit down at the table.

GIFTS

This is not always easy. Should you or should you not bring a gift to your host? I think that you should. It is a courtesy, a thank-you in advance. It should not be anything too extravagant, but it should be enough to bring a smile to their face.

Flowers, wine and chocolates seem to be the most usual. Just give a thought to whether they will be appropriate or not. If you know that your host has diabetes, would chocolates be a good idea? If it is likely to be a dry, alcohol-free occasion then wine will perhaps be an embarrassment. If you know that your host or their partner has hay fever, then you might need to think again about bringing flowers.

Originality is always a good card to play. How about a CD, a book, or a jar of honey?

THE PRE-PRANDIAL PERIOD

This means before the meal. It is a medical expression, yet it is worth knowing about because it is always a snippet of information that you can talk about at a diner party.

The pre-prandial period begins from the minute you arrive, greet your host and are shown or are directed where to go. It is likely to be into a sitting room where others may already have arrived. It is the host's duty to introduce you.

It is your duty to greet each person according to the accepted social behaviour relating to the setting. I am assuming that this is a Western-style dinner party, in which case a man should shake other male's hands and air-kiss the females. A woman may choose to air-kiss members of both sexes.

Then the talking begins. This is the opportunity to get to know the host and the other guests.

Drinks may be on hand, but it is bad form to quaff them down and ask for more, or to indicate that you need another. It will give the impression that you are nervous and need Dutch courage or that you are over-fond of alcohol. Pace yourself.

Be conscious also of using the drinking action as a nervous gesture. People can hide behind their glass. Really, in this phase of the dinner party the less that you raise the glass to your lips the better. It shows that you are a controlled person and that you are more interested in the other people and what they have to say than in the contents of the drink.

Use the openers in Chapter 6 and see if you can get a sense of people's representational systems. Are they visuals, auditories or kinaesthetics? If you can pick up on this then try to reflect that in the way you talk to them.

There will be lots of opportunity to find out about the others. Remember, if the conversation gets strained or a pregnant pause occurs, then ask an open question. You can also comment about the surroundings, or express approval of clothes, hair, jewellery.

I will talk about body language in the next chapter on mingling. This can have relevance if you are standing and talking or sitting down comfortably.

Strategy

When a pregnant pause seems likely, ask a question. Remember location, reason for being there, current affairs, the future.

THE MEAL ITSELF

Exactly what sort of dinner party it is will have a bearing on how the table is set, or even on whether you will have the opportunity to sit down at a table. If it is a buffet then it is a much more mobile event and we will touch on that in Chapter 9, on 'Mingling'.

A sit-down meal offers lots of opportunity for civilized conversation. There are so many variables, of course. The shape and size of the table, the number of guests sitting down and the background music, noise or banter that you have to deal with.

The seating arrangement may be haphazard or deliberately planned. If there are enough people of both sexes then most people aim at male, female, male, female seating pattern. If it is two couples, then it is good to have opposite couples and opposite sexes facing each other. Yet it all depends on the host and the structure of the party. All of these variables are outwith the control of the guest and they should be looked on as delightful challenges to their talking ability, not as a form of social torture that has to be endured at all costs.

It is supposed to be fun, remember.

Do

There are a few things that you should aim to do. These might sound obvious, yet a surprising number of people do not observe the niceties:

▶ *Sit politely and wait your turn to be served. Females are served first, males last.*
▶ *Wait until everyone has been served, then wait until your host is ready to eat.*
▶ *If there is a daunting row of cutlery either side of your plate, start on the outside and work inwards.*
▶ *Be prepared to pass things to your fellow guests.*
▶ *Be complementary to the host about the table arrangement, the décor, the meal, the drink (if any) and the company.*
▶ *Be prepared to say grace if asked – but only if asked. Suggesting to say a religious grace when eating with people who are not of any faith may be a conversation-stopper and the cause of tension.*

- ▶ Be prepared to say 'amen' if someone does say grace.
- ▶ Be ready to open a conversation.
- ▶ Be ready to reply to questions. Take small mouthfuls so that you can finish them easily without talking with food in your mouth.
- ▶ Do use your napkin to dab your mouth.
- ▶ Talk clearly and pitch the volume of your voice so that you can be heard. You must not be thought of as a mumbler.

Do not

Similarly these are things you should not do:

- ▶ Never, ever, talk with your mouth full. It does not look nice.
- ▶ Never, ever, eat with your mouth open. It is unpleasant for others to see the macerated contents of your mouth.
- ▶ Do not pick your teeth unless there are toothpicks available.
- ▶ Do not lean too close to someone to talk, since you are eating and you should be mindful of your breath.
- ▶ Do not make inappropriate remarks about your host or any of the guests.
- ▶ Do not crack inappropriate jokes.

THE CONVERSATION MAY FOLLOW THE COURSES

You can really think of a meal having three parts – starter, main and sweet. It is not a bad idea to think of the table conversation as mirroring that. The starter will often tend to follow the cocktail chatter or small talk of the pre-prandial period. It is when some of the later guests may be catching up and getting to know all of the others.

The main course will tend to be when people are ready for more solid conversation. Indeed, either the host will serve the main topic of discussion or one of the guests will bring up a subject that is worthy of their full attention after their appetite for conversation, discussion and debate has been whetted by the starter conversations.

This is where your preparations can come in handy. Either you can be the one to introduce the main topic, or your research will have given you information to keep the conversation going.

By the time the sweet comes you may have exhausted the main topic and you are then just rounding things off with some sweet topics. Here again your researches may hold you in good stead.

POST-PRANDIAL PERIOD

In the old days the ladies withdrew to the drawing room for tea or coffee and light conversation while the men remained around the table and smoked cigars and drank port, while they discussed heavier matters like the economy or politics.

You might like to drop this little snippet of information in, that the drawing room is a shortened version of 'withdrawing' room. It refers to this habit of the ladies withdrawing to leave the men. After a while the men would join them, once they had sorted out the problems of the world.

That was the etiquette of days gone by. It is a good thing that such customs have changed. Now everyone tends to move through to the sitting room for coffees and general small talk. Here you can use the techniques of Chapter 7 to keep the conversation going, until, at a reasonable time, it is appropriate to start closing down.

No one ever wants to be the first to leave for some reason. Yet once someone has made it clear that it is their intention to do so, others will follow suit. If you feel you wish to be the first person, then there is no reason to feel embarrassed. Someone has to do it and others will be grateful that they are being spared from that role.

Top Tip
Never show that you are keen to get away, and be careful not to overstay your welcome.

9

Mingling

At parties, social events, business meetings and conferences there are lots of times when people will be milling around. Depending on the circumstances people use them to network, make friends, gain information, or even to flirt and find partners. They all have boundaries, of course, yet some people are so comfortable with themselves and their ability to communicate that they may take the chance to cross those boundaries.

If that sounds shocking, it is because you are not the type of person to cross boundaries, to breach codes of etiquette. That is good; there is no need for you to do so. Just be comfortable being you.

Yet, as I have indicated so many times in this book, many people are not at all comfortable in their own skin. They may feel awkward about themselves and about their ability to talk and integrate. Finding oneself in the middle of a crowd of strangers may be one of their worst nightmares. Yet it need not be and it should not be. The truth is that every person is as good as every other person. If they would just learn to hold their head up high and mingle.

It is not difficult actually.

When you enter a crowded room what do you do?

There are a number of different behaviours that one tends to see. It is not quite as clear-cut as this, perhaps, yet these are definite patterns that you will see. Each person may behave slightly differently depending on the type of gathering and how they perceive their role and how they are feeling at that time. In other words everyone has several ways that they might act, but they will tend to have one behaviour that is their most natural, if not exactly their favoured, behaviour.

I liken these behaviours to ice-skating and the room to an ice rink.

'I MAKE MY WAY STRAIGHT TO WHERE THE ACTION IS'

This person likes the limelight and they want to be where the focus of attention is. They enter, look round, see where the centre or the hub of interest seems to be, then they make their way in that direction. They are probably naturally adept at talking and will chat to folk on their way, but it will be clear to one and all that they are heading eventually towards the hub. They will get there and they will enjoy taking their share of the limelight.

Ego is never a problem for this type of person, whom I call the figure skater. It is as if they glide easily, performing whatever manoeuvres are needed in order to work the rink.

There is absolutely nothing wrong with being a figure skater. They take the light away from others who are less happy to be caught in it.

'I HAPPILY FLOAT AROUND THE ROOM'

This person does just that. They go in and they mingle. They have no obvious target and do not crave the limelight, but they are happy to meet and talk to anyone they encounter on their way.

They do not have to know them, but can, if they find themselves in the vicinity of a new group, make contact.

I call this person the mover. They are happy to move about on a crowded rink, weaving in and out wherever they need to.

The mover is often the person that people envy, for they go where they want, perhaps not attracting the same amount of attention as the figure skater, yet they are comfortable in their easy ability.

'I SPOT SOMEONE I KNOW AND I MAKE FOR THEM FIRST'

This person will enter and look for people that are known and considered safe. Then he or she will home in on them and stop and chat for a while, all the time seeing who else is in the room. They do not like making complex moves, don't like to have to travel far, but when they have built up their confidence and lost their nerves they will skate to the next group.

I liken this type to the developing skater. They have some comfort in their ability to go a little way. They feel comfortable going from a group of people they know to other groups that they know. They are less likely to spark up a conversation with others themselves, but probably will be OK if someone talks to them.

'I GO STRAIGHT FOR THE SIDE OF THE ROOM WHERE THERE IS SOMEONE I KNOW I CAN TALK TO'

This person is like the skater who heads straight for the wall of the rink and latches onto someone they know with whom they can then perhaps venture further afield, provided they hold their hand.

I call this person the beginning skater. They will manage to skate to the side of the rink, but have little confidence to go off on their own. They need a safe and helping hand. Someone they can talk to.

'I HEAD STRAIGHT FOR SOMEWHERE THAT I CAN BECOME INVISIBLE'

This person probably has social anxiety and hates social occasions. They literally try to merge into the background. If there is a buffet they may load their plate, take a drink and head for a corner where they can get their head down so that no one can see them to engage them in conversation, because they won't look at anyone.

I call this person the very visible invisible skater. The truth is that they are so fearful of showing that they are not adept that they behave in precisely the manner that makes them very visible. They are giving out signals of fear and also signals that they do not want to interact.

'I REALLY DON'T FEEL LIKE TALKING, BUT IF SOMEONE TALKS TO ME THAT'S OK'

This type of person is just shy. They can talk if they want, or if they can be persuaded to. They may even enjoy it. Indeed, they may actually have the ability to be the figure skater. I call this type the reluctant skater, for obvious reasons.

Most people will in fact relate to one of these skater types. Generally most people would like to be either the figure skater or the mover. They would just like to be a bit more adept and a bit more relaxed in getting around the room.

You can if you just use some simple strategies.

Personal space and proxemics

I am sure you will have heard about this. Personal space is the area of space around you that you psychologically regard as yours. People are territorial about their personal space and do not like to have it invaded by others. By and large it is egg-shaped, being conical behind one and extending outwards in front of them like the bottom of an egg.

The concept of personal space was developed by the anthropologist Edward T. Hall (1914–2009). He had based his work on that of Heini Hediger (1908–92), a Swiss zoologist who had studied the behaviour of zoo animals. Hediger had distinguished a number of areas and distances surrounding an animal, each of which had different significance. The flight zone was the area around it which would trigger an escape reaction if it was encroached upon by another creature. The critical distance was the area in which it would defend itself or attack. The personal distance was the distance it kept between itself and another of its kind that it did not wish to contact, and social distance was the distance between two of the same species if they wished to communicate.

Edward Hall observed people in order to see whether these areas and distances had relevance to humans. He concluded that the

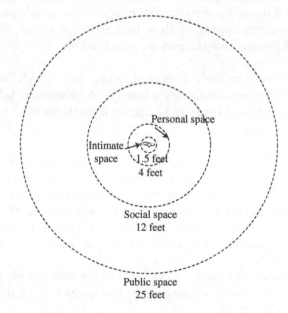

Personal space

Intimate space
1.5 feet
4 feet

Social space
12 feet

Public space
25 feet

Figure 9.1 The four proxemic spaces.

flight zone and the critical distance had been eliminated from human behaviour, but that personal space and social distance were highly important, but variable depending upon culture, gender, social standing, individual psychology, personal preference and circumstance. He coined the name proxemics to describe the study of measurable distances between people as they interact. We will be looking at this in both this chapter and later in Chapter 10 on 'Flirtation'.

It is germane to understanding why some people have difficulty with mingling. They perceive it is a violation of their personal space and they do not feel comfortable letting people whom they do not know well get too close to them. It is not the whole of the matter, but it is a significant factor.

In his 1966 book *The Hidden Dimension* Hall described four distinct areas or personal reaction bubbles that surround the individual. Essentially, the relationship one individual has with another will define the distance within which they would permit another person to approach. These four proxemic spaces, together with the distances from the person, are as follows:

Intimate space – this is the reserve of lovers, close friends and relatives. As the name indicates it is reserved for intimate behaviour including touching, kissing and hugging. It measures from 0 to 18 inches (0–46 cm).

Personal distance – *this is the comfortable distance for personal conversations. It can be quite keenly demarcated and someone can feel intimidated if it is slightly impinged upon, yet they can feel rejected and nonplussed if someone stays well beyond it. It ranges from 18 inches to 4 feet (46–122 cm) for most Westerners, although as we shall see there are cultural differences.*

Social distance – *in day-to-day life, talking with people in shops at business meetings, etc. The range is 4–12 feet (122 cm–3.7 m).*

Public distance – *this is the public speaking distance. If giving a speech or a lecture people feel most comfortable when their audience is not too close; otherwise they may feel inhibited. This is an important point if you are giving presentations or lectures. The range is 12 feet (3.7 m) and above.*

Edward Hall also looked at these areas and distances in relationship to cultures. He found that Latin countries tend to have a smaller personal space than do the British or the Americans. Nordic countries have a larger personal space.

Interestingly, at events such as international medical conferences, which the author has attended, he has noticed this tendency. Delegates of one culture may tend to advance into the personal space of delegates from another culture. Gradually this advancing–retreating behaviour results in the more reserved delegates being pushed gradually towards the periphery or towards the centre, depending upon where they had started. I should emphasize now that this is entirely an anecdotal piece of information, based on observation alone.

PERSONAL SPACE SIZE

The size of the personal space is not easy to measure, but for people in the UK it is about 28–30 inches (71–76 cm) in front of them, about 24 inches (61 cm) at the side and only about 14–16 inches (36–41 cm) behind. It is egg-shaped.

Obviously the type of event may have a bearing upon the personal space size. If you are at a business meeting then it will possibly enlarge, so that it becomes closer to that of the social distance. If you are at a party it will probably get much smaller, since the whole atmosphere is different and people expect to get closer.

Social status is another thing that can affect personal space. In general, the higher up any hierarchy someone is to an individual, the more reluctant one is to encroach on their space.

TACTILITY

This is an interesting one because some people are decidedly more tactile than others. A tactile person likes to reach out and touch hands and arms and they like also to be touched.

Other people who tend to use visual and auditory representational systems more frequently are probably less comfortable with tactility, until they get to know someone well and signal that they are willing to let people in.

Strategy

Always be conscious of an individual's representational system. Visuals and auditory types are less likely to appreciate being touched than kinaesthetics.

BODY POSITIONING

This is often very revealing in the context of mingling. You will notice it in any gathering of people. People tend to position themselves in such a way that they are either face on and very open, meaning that they are amenable to conversation, or they angle themselves to indicate various degrees of caution or reluctance to talk.

In proxemics the shoulder axis is the way to assess someone's openness or otherwise. Imagine a line through their shoulders and its relationship to you, the mingler. If they are parallel to your own shoulders, that is zero degrees. If they are standing slightly at an angle, then that indicates reserve and you have to get them to open up. Greater degrees of angle up to ninety degrees, where they are speaking over their shoulder to you suggest that they do really not want to talk. You are almost being given the cold shoulder.

The art of mingling

The very first thing that you should do is to implant it into your mind that most people will be quite happy to talk to someone at a meeting, conference and party as long as they don't have to make the first move. You yourself possibly feel relieved in such circumstances when someone introduces himself to you.

Strategy

Resolve to be the first to introduce yourself at the next social occasion when you don't know everyone. Just go up to someone that you do not know, smile at them and say, 'Hello, I am.... What's our name?'

You will soon be talking and the chances are that they will be grateful to you for breaking the ice.

Suppose it is a business meeting. There is a good chance that most people will be wearing a name badge. Always make a point of looking at the badge and registering the name. That is a gift! Accept the gift of their name and use it straight away in your introduction.

Some people dislike wearing name badges and at the start of a conference secret them in a pocket or pin them behind a lapel so that they cannot be seen. They need help to mingle and that is a good cue for you. There really is nothing wrong with you introducing yourself and then asking them for their name. Nine times out of ten they will respond warmly and excuse themselves by saying that they hate name badges. That is an immediate opportunity to ask why and start the conversation.

You should wear your name badge at a meeting and give some thought as to where to pin it. Don't pin it on the top of your trousers or onto a dress at waist height. This causes your fellow attendee to look down. The best place in on your right side at about lapel height. Thus they can see your badge and see your name as you shake hands.

Breaking into a clique

At cocktail parties or conferences where people are on their feet moving about, it may sometimes feel awkward when you approach two or three people and find them deep in conversation. You may not feel that you can break in, or they may seem quite exclusive and not give any indication that they have seen you, or that they want to acknowledge your presence.

If it is a party, then you should not feel inhibited. The whole point of a party is that people should be able to interact with everyone else there. So, there is nothing wrong in just standing, listening and waiting for an opportunity to say something. The vast majority of people will notice, and they will not be so rude as to ignore you. When they turn and smile, then you smile back, introduce yourself and move forward into the group. Likewise, if someone approaches a group that you are in, move to make room and show that they are welcome.

It is a good idea to be ready with something to add. For example:

'I heard that you were talking about…. Well, that is so interesting, because I had an experience with….'

Two or three people in a clique can be the hardest to join in with if they do not know you. With four or more there will be less dynamics going on and you will find you are quickly assimilated. Yet most people will open the group up if you approach them.

Enjoy your mingling!

Mingle whenever you can.

10

Flirtation

> *There's a language in her eye, her cheek, her lip; Nay, her*
> *foot speaks. Her wanton spirits look out at every joint and*
> *motive of her body.*
>
> William Shakespeare, *Troilus and Cressida*

Flirtation is normal. Except in a few very restrictive societies and
situations, nunneries and monasteries being obvious examples,
people in all walks of life and of all ages enjoy flirtation. It almost
seems to be an innate form of behaviour. It is our way of making
contact with another person that one finds attractive and
communicating that feeling to them.

Yet although flirtation seems to be an innate or natural behaviour
it has to be said that it does not come naturally to everyone. There
are many shy, unconfident people who are so fearful of rejection
that they put up barriers, blush at any approach to them and
consequently avoid social situations. They may envy those people
who are able to flirt with abandon, who seem able to enter any
social situation and just wing it.

Well, as with other areas of talking that we have looked at
in this book, there is no need to be fearful. Anyone can flirt
if they understand something of the unwritten code of flirtation.
Effectively, go in with a sensible game plan and you will open up a
whole new and enjoyable part of your life.

An innate behaviour

There is of course good biological reason why flirtation should be an instinctive behaviour. For one thing attracting a sexual partner is an important prelude to reproduction in order to protect the species. At a more personal biological level, so evolutionary biologists would tell us, we are attracted to individuals with whom we wish to mate in order to perpetuate our own DNA.

So much for the basic instinctive drive. Science can take a lot of the magic out of life, since protecting one's DNA or maintaining the human species is not uppermost in most of our minds most of the time. Indeed, gay men and women may have no desire to reproduce, yet have a perfectly healthy desire to express their feelings to people they feel attracted to. This section has just as much relevance to them.

HARMLESS FLIRTATION

This is fun flirtation. It may amount to no more than harmless banter between workmates, acquaintances or strangers at a party. It is pleasurable chit-chat that can lighten the mood, boost egos and help with morale. People mingle in all sorts of social situations and, provided the situation is appropriate, harmless flirtation is almost an expected part of life.

Both men and women do it in the course of their normal life. Indeed, it is likely that most people will flirt with someone at least once a week and in many cases at least once a day.

There are boundaries that one should be aware of, however. These are not clear-cut at all, and a lot depends upon one's ability to read situations. At work, for example, harmless flirtation can pass a boundary and be misconstrued as sexual harassment, particularly by men towards female colleagues.

If one of the people involved in harmless flirtation is married or in a relationship, then there is potential danger for both parties. Care must be taken about giving out the wrong signals. Similarly, you have to be wary of misconstruing harmless flirting as an invitation for a deeper physical relationship.

MEANINGFUL FLIRTATION

This is the sort of flirtation that takes place when people strike up conversations with meaningful intent. It is flirting with the aim of getting to know the other person and possibly beginning some sort of a relationship with them.

Members of both sexes may initiate flirtation. Many men think that it is their responsibility to be the initiators and equate flirtation with 'chatting up'. They may vie with each other to come up with the best pick-up line. Many will have success with even the corniest of openers:

'I love your smile. I'd love to see it at the breakfast table.'
'Give me three good reasons why I can't buy you a drink?'

Crass? Of course they are. Such openers do not succeed by virtue of their wit; it is simply that they have been used on someone who may be open to engaging with the chancer, regardless of what they say. It is likely that they will only be open to such openers if they have had some alcohol. And that is not unlikely considering that so much flirtation takes place in social situations where alcohol is flowing.

Indeed, most women dislike such opening lines. Research has shown that women find them too aggressive or simply too banal. Girls laugh among themselves at the witless and guileless pick-up lines that they have been spun.

The simple truth is that in flirtation, as with all types of human communication and interaction, people are influenced more by body language and by your tone and the way you put things across rather than by what you actually say. The content of your speech is still very important, of course; it is just that when you want to make an impact you need to be aware of these other factors.

Strategy

STRATEGY

Prepare to ditch banal opening pick-up lines.

Love chemistry

Let me digress a little, since it is important to know that we do in fact behave according to how we feel.

People usually think of the heart as being the organ of the body associated with attraction and love. In fact, according to research from neuroscientists in both the USA and the UK, love is actually more likely to be in the head than in the heart. That is to say, research has discovered various changes in the brain that take place when one falls in love.

Scientists at University College London and colleagues at the Albert Einstein College of Medicine in New York studied brain scans of people who admitted to being in the full flush of love, or even 'madly in love'. By monitoring infatuated students they have found that photographs of their loved one would cause blood to rush to four small areas of the brain. On the brain scan these areas literally light up. This does not happen when photographs of even close friends are shown.

These areas of the brain are ones associated with emotion and pleasure. Two of the areas are rich in receptors for dopamine, a principal neurotransmitter in the brain.

Courting behaviour

It may sound trite to talk about the birds and the bees, but there is a serious point. All species have been shown to have courting behaviour and mating behaviour. So do humans. Yet people do not like to think that their behaviour is in any way animal-like. Certainly in the area of courting they like to imagine that it is a matter of skill and know-how.

Well the truth is somewhere between the two. It is a matter of know-how, in that a lot of it is innate behaviour, and it is also something that can be developed into a skill. Some people are very good at it while others feel quite reserved and inept. It doesn't necessarily have as much to do with physical attractiveness either. Some beautiful people may fail to gain a partner simply because they put people off by giving out the wrong signals.

Birds, bees, educated fleas, as the great lyricist Cole Porter informed us, all fall in love. They perform their own courting behaviour in order to attract a partner, then they mate. The courting behaviour does not always work, of course. It will tend to, but the whole aim is to find the best mate in order to have the best chance of producing the best and fittest progeny. That is the Darwinian and evolutionary biology view, at any rate.

We humans like to think that we are at the top of the evolutionary ladder. The selected species. As such we imagine that we have left the lower types of behaviour behind us, so that we live our lives according to cold logic. Clearly that is nonsense. It is a deception that we foist upon our children from the youngest age. People still behave in the ways that are innate. The problem lies in the fact that we have become socialized to the degree that we suppress our natural ways of behaving and forget how to read the natural signals. In addition, because each of us can only ever experience our own unique life, we place ourselves at the centre of our own emotional universe. That means that if we are rebuffed, we find it hard to come to terms with. It is a memory that will be remembered by your inner critic and may be used against you the next time that you put your head above the courting parapet.

So the thing to do is to accept and rejoice in the fact that you have innate abilities to court a partner. Just remember that socialization may have suppressed that natural exuberance, *joie de vivre* and your ability to court. Let us therefore revisit the pattern of courting and then we can look at some strategies you can put in place in order to read and give out the right signals. You will hopefully then find that your innate courting talents come to the fore.

Top Tip

Men are not good at reading signals. They are more likely to interpret a friendly signal as a sexual interest signal. The reason is the testosterone hormone.

The five phases of courtship

Whether we are talking about animals and birds or humans there seem to be five progressive phases of courtship. Some of them may be bypassed if mutual attraction is strong and the conditions are right.

These five phases seem to be followed by people all over the world, regardless of culture. There may well be cultural differences, in the way that something is done, yet the core phases are the same.

1 ATTRACTING ATTENTION

This is where eye contact is made and held.

In the animal kingdom this is the showing of feathers, or the start of a strut. Humans see someone that they find attractive, then they begin to subtly, or not so subtly, find ways to attract attention. The aim is to be eye-catching. If eye contact is made and held, and this holding of eye contact is the important thing, then phase two may be entered.

2 REACTION

This is where people signal that they have accepted the attraction. It usually starts with a smile.

I have emphasized the importance of smiling throughout the book. It is of fundamental importance in day-to-day life. In flirtation it is essential to smile nicely, since a smile is often one of the very first things that starts the process of flirtation.

There is usually an opening smile from one person and a reciprocating smile from the other. It can trigger the whole amazing chemistry of attraction. The thing is, can you tell anything from those smiles about whether you are likely to click? Indeed you can.

There are four ways that you can tell the difference between a natural smile and a forced or a polite smile:

1 *A natural smile is accompanied by smile wrinkles near the eyes. They are absent in the polite smile.*
2 *There is a time lag in a polite smile. It is not instantaneous, but follows a thought, such as 'I had better smile' or ' I had better be polite'.*
3 *Look at the shape of the person's face. A natural smile is symmetrical, since all of the facial muscles that make you smile have been triggered off naturally. A polite smile will be slightly*

asymmetrical, because the smile is forced so the dominant side muscles will contract more than the non-dominant side.

4 *A natural smile varies and changes as you look at it. A polite smile will be static and mask-like and seems to be held by the smiler.*

As I mentioned earlier in the book, the mirror is your friend. It is worth knowing how your face moves, how you make facial expressions and how you look as you talk. If you want to become successful at flirtation, then you need to study how your face moves and how you yourself move. Talking, conversing and flirting are dependent upon making yourself seem totally natural. And paradoxically that may mean that you need to do a little practising in front of the mirror.

Be aware that there are certain signs that indicate you are *not* being encouraged – especially:

▶ *lack of eye contact*
▶ *unsmiling poker face*
▶ *closed and unresponsive body language.*

As long as you have not had these negative signals, then the next phase beckons.

3 PREENING

This body language is so important. Some of it is almost involuntary. For example both parties tend to pull the stomach in and lift the shoulders to be their full height and as slim and elegant as they can be.

Other moves may seem more contrived, yet they will also be innate. Females will tend to make movements that demonstrate willingness to be submissive. They may tilt the head, a gesture that exposes the neck. Or they will show the inner surfaces of their wrists and arms. Men may thrust their chest out to demonstrate power, lift the chin to show masterfulness.

Strategy

Combine a smile with an appropriate body movement to make a bigger impact.

Both may play with their hair. Women may raise a hand to tidy their hair. When they use the opposite hand to reach over their head to move hair on the side of the head they are effectively flaunting their hair.

Trichologically challenged men may stroke their shaven cheeks with an upward move of the closed hand, producing a slight rasping noise to demonstrate their masculinity in another way.

Body position is important. Essentially, the front of the body is directed towards the other. Legs may be crossed towards the other person. The whole posture may be leaned towards them as well, so that complete attention is given.

Body movements may be introduced. Rhythmic swaying, rocking are warm, friendly movements and are showing openness.

Below are summaries of typical preening behaviours.

Females

▶ *Tilt head to expose neck*
▶ *Eye position. Tilting the head down so that you can look upwards is elfin and highly attractive to others.*
▶ *Rotate hands to expose inner surface of wrist or arm*
▶ *Touch hair with opposite hand*
▶ *Position body to face person*
▶ *Cross legs*
▶ *Foot waggling or shoe dangling*
▶ *Body swaying*
▶ *Use accessories like jewellery. Touching them emphasizes adornments*

4 TALKING

You may feel this is the crux of the matter, because it is often the part that people feel most ill at ease with. Bear in mind that the tone of voice is important. Varying the tone, without being crass or suggestive, tends to impact on people.

Smiling intermittently is also good as long as it is appropriate. You have to get the balance between smiling as a means of subtly emphasizing what you were saying and just simply leering.

It is a good thing to abandon the idea of chat-up lines. Instead show your maturity by simply starting small talk. If you can master the art of small talk then you are armed to begin and keep a conversation going. It is as simple as that.

5 TOUCHING

By now you are close enough to touch.

A simple straightforward handshake at the start is non-threatening. An air-kiss is only appropriate if you know the person or if it is an accepted part of protocol.

As the ice is broken then a touch of the hand or a touch on the arm is a positive sign. A touch to the wrist may be taken as a positive warm move. In general, men need to be careful about being first to touch. Indeed, although it may seem surprising, females tend to be the first to break this barrier.

After that, it very much depends upon how the people wish to develop their 'relationship'.

_____

Asking someone out

This can fill people with dread. It is normal to be apprehensive because no one likes to be rejected. Yet if it is phrased well then it need not be a rejection issue. Regard it as an invitation that you are giving someone.

While we are on the subject, there is no problem why a female cannot ask a male out on a date. This is the twenty-first century and the social mores of the last century are long gone, in terms of asking someone for a date, at any rate.

The situations in which two people meet are legion. Strangers may exchange glances across a crowded room, across the length of an underground carriage, as neighbouring workers, or in social places such as sports clubs, gyms or parties of one sort or another.

To start, whom do you ask out? It might sound a banal question, but it really depends on your lifestyle. Whom do you meet? Do you belong to any clubs where there are people you may be attracted to, or who may be attracted to you? Do you go clubbing or visit bars? If you do, do you go on your own or with a friend or in a larger group?

For the tongue-tied and terrified person asking someone out can be a daunting thing to do. Work is often one of the easiest places to meet someone. It is also a place where a lot of banter and flirting goes on. That may be your best bet. Indeed, there may be someone there that has been waiting ages for you to at last pick up the courage and ask.

Conventions are often good places where people are coming with shared interests. Art festivals, science fiction events, sports tournaments and competitions may also offer opportunities. Look for signals.

SO WHAT DO YOU SAY TO GET STARTED?

No one except the brave is going to go up to someone and just ask them out. That is too bold. People like to talk first so that they can assess each other. What you do is open up your small talk. You will already have a substantial repertoire of things to talk about. Choose the appropriate questions and initiate a conversation.

This is the same for everyone regardless of their sex. Be prepared to respond with your small talk if the other person has started the conversation. Then keep it going. It may not be appropriate to ask someone out on that occasion, but as you know you can close with rejoinders to keep in contact. A phone number so that you can call or text to arrange a meeting or the modern version of the old-fashioned telegram, an email address so you can shoot off an email.

You should have some ideas of where you would like to ask the other person out to. It is good to have an idea of a specific place or event rather than just a vague 'Would you like to come out with me?' A lot depends on your personality, but do make sure that you are going to go somewhere that you will have plenty of opportunity for conversation. The cinema is great if you are both film buffs, but meeting, going straight to a movie and watching the film before talking may not be the best way of forging a relationship. It is a good thing to do after you have already done that. Dinner, a drink, a bar, a party, they are all places where you can chat. Concerts, exhibitions and theatre and film may demand a lot of focus on something else rather than on the two of you.

A sporting activity is another possibility. Bowling, badminton, tennis, squash or golf are all possibilities. You just have to work out how competitive you both are and whether it would be OK to go all out and wipe the other person off the court, course or lane.

Are you a good loser or a bad loser? A date like that may tell you much about each other; it is up to you whether you risk it or not.

Think also about the way that you ask. Get the balance right.

'I am going to see the wrestling on Saturday. Do you want to come along?'
That is a bit too matter-of-fact.

'Would you like to maybe go somewhere for a meal, if you're not too busy?'
That is too unsure. You are expecting rejection.

'Would you like to come and have dinner with some friends of mine?'
What sort of invitation is that? Is it just to be a dinner partner? Will the person want to make conversation with other people as well as with you? It is a bit ambiguous.

Strategy

Start with small talk and get to know each other. If you move on to a potential date then aim to be enthusiastic whenever you are asking and also if you have been asked. Don't give the impression that you 'don't mind'. It seems as if you haven't had a better offer.

The date

People enjoy complements. Never more so than on that first date. Don't be crass; be subtle, unless you are both of a brasher type of personality. It is perfectly acceptable on a date to complement people on their appearance. You are in a different situation from those first tentative small talk chats. One of you has asked and the other has agreed to go somewhere and there you are, both about to enjoy yourselves and both anticipating and hoping that it is going to lead to a second date and the start of a relationship. Or, on the other hand, to just have a pleasant time and make a mutual decision not to progress further.

So you carry on with small talk, but it is good to start picking up on things that you have talked about before. This shows that you were listening and that you were interested.

'I was really interested in that story you told me. It made me think about...'
Here you can demonstrate that they made an impression on you and that you can relate a similar experience.

'I think it is so cool that you like ...'
Here you can show mutual interests, or your willingness to find out about their interests.

'When you told me about...I wanted to say...'
Now you can say something pertinent to that chat. This shows that you did not want to press on that first occasion.

The date inevitably moves you through the phases of courtship. You will both expect it to move through talking to touching. There will be a shortening of the distance between you as you demonstrate your mutual attraction. Look out for body language, detect signals, but my male readers should make sure that they don't read too much into things!

Kissing certainly moves you to a different level. Not just in terms of how you behave, but in terms of what will be happening in your brains. Different neurotransmitters and hormones will start to be released, as I mentioned in the chemistry of love section. If you are both firing these off then you will be all too aware that things are going well.

You may find that you are enjoying the other person's company and that you want to see more of them. You may well find that you have really moved into the realm of intimacy. Here, of course, body language and behaviour, essentially how you demonstrate your attraction will probably play more of a part than verbal communication, although endearments are likely to add to the emotional charge that you both feel.

Pillow talk

The closer people get to one another the more likely they are to open up. After making love people tend to lower their defences and are more willing than ever to talk about themselves, their feelings, their desires and their secrets. The movie industry makes a lot of this with the bedroom scenes that pepper and pep up films.

So too are the security forces around the world, who use spies to infiltrate organizations, to seduce and get people into the sack in order to tap the secrets that come out in pillow talk.

You may not be a spy with ulterior motives in sharing a bed with someone. And you may not be someone with state or other secrets that you need to hold back. You may be just someone enjoying the physical side of a new relationship. The thing is to be aware of this tendency to let your guard down and to let out a lot about yourself. It is possible that you may regret telling too much too soon.

Then again, you may just enhance your relationship.

11

It's how you tell them

Something which has never occurred since time immemorial;
a young woman did not fart in her husband's lap.

Ancient Sumeria, 1900 BC, reputedly the oldest
recorded joke in the world

You may not find that joke very amusing. Then again, it may have
had you in stitches. It is out of time, for one thing, yet it shows that
even in ancient days people enjoyed risqué jokes. It has two very
interesting components: firstly it implies decorum or what would
be an unfeminine thing to do, and secondly it is about passing
flatus, which people always seem to find funny, especially if they
enjoy toilet jokes.

Perhaps if it was said with an accent, or if it was said after you had
talked about ancient Sumeria, or about the relationships between
men and women over the centuries, then it may seem funnier.
Jokes have to be in context, after all. A joke just dropped into a
conversation may or may not make someone laugh. It depends on
several things, not least of them being how it is told.

Some people seem to be naturals at telling jokes. They seem to
have a fund of them that they can drop into most conversations.
As a result they get a reputation for being funny people who are
good for a laugh and who know how to make you laugh. If they
are really good they may even have a go at stand-up comedy. Who
knows, if they are talented they may even make a living out of it.

Most people, however, are not particularly good at telling jokes. They tend to have just three or four, they tell them badly, spoil their own punchlines or, worse, they tell them at the most inappropriate times.

Yet being able to tell a few jokes may be one of the best things that a tongue-tied type of person ought to cultivate. It is something that you can learn to do, but like most things that are worth doing well it just takes practice. There is that word that I have used so many times in this book – practice.

It is true. You can learn to tell jokes and you can make people laugh. If you are not naturally a funny person then don't expect to suddenly transform yourself into a comic genius. However, you can learn to tell anecdotes and simple jokes that will make your fellows laugh – if you learn the techniques. Just as actors rehearse their lines, comedians rehearse their jokes. They don't just appear out of nowhere. They are worked at and polished.

You can do it too.

ACT

This is a book about talking, yet you will notice that I have repeatedly mentioned acting and practising. I make no bones about this because you do need to practise any activity in order to make it become second nature.

The ACT here, however, is an acronym for three important things you need to be aware of when telling a joke. These are:

1 *Audience*
2 *Confidence*
3 *Timing.*

AUDIENCE

This is fundamental. It is all about the audience you are going to perform in front of. You may not think that your joke telling merits the word 'audience', yet it does. An audience means the person or people that are listening to your performance. That may be your partner on a first date, a group standing with you at the bar, a smart group round a dinner table or a meeting of the local Bible discussion group.

You see the point? It is vitally important that you tell only jokes that are appropriate for the audience at that moment in time. A ribald joke may be OK for the guys at the pub, but it would be likely to make people blush at the Bible group, and it could very well make the first date your last date with that person.

If there is any doubt about appropriateness then don't joke.

Inappropriate humour

Sarcasm – no one ever actually finds it funny. It merely marks the sarcastic joker as someone to be wary of.

Racism – is never funny. Someone will be offended and you should be ashamed of making such jokes.

Sexism – has no place in the modern world.

Mocking *beliefs*.

Mocking *minority groups*.

Mocking people with *disabilities* of any sort.

Think before you launch into any joke. If it is not something you would tell your parents or your nephew or niece then don't tell it. There are other jokes you can and should be able to use.

CONFIDENCE

If you are going to tell a joke then you need to deliver it with panache. Be confident in the way you deliver it. This means not prefacing it with a phrase like 'I heard a joke. Bear with me, because I'm not very good at jokes or accents, but here goes...'

How would you react to that? You expect a poor delivery, a poor performance. You are not likely to laugh other than by forcing a polite laugh.

The same thing goes for smiling or laughing at your own joke before you get to the punch line. It just makes you seem inept and you are better not putting yourself into that position.

I said in Chapter 5 ('Appreciate Your Voice') that learning some patter is a useful way of starting small talk. It is a very good thing to do when joke telling. It needs to be crisp and smooth as though it trips off your tongue. Only practice will do that.

TIMING

Good jokes depend on good timing. Timing sets a good joker apart from an indifferent one.

If your idea of a good joke lies just in the content of the joke, then think again. Get a joke book and just read a joke out loud to some of the family. They may smile. They may even laugh, but they are unlikely to fall in fits of hysterics unless you tell it well. That means that you need to deliver it well, emphasizing certain words, building up an atmosphere and then delivering the punch line in just the right way.

Jokes depend on twists, just as a good crime novel or thriller does. You have to build the atmosphere, perhaps with a bit of acting, then mislead them as you talk your way through the joke.

Then you pause for a moment and then drop the punchline without any show that you find it amusing. That is timing.

The punchline has to hit them. The pause helps to heighten the tension, and all jokes have to build a little tension or expectation or they are going to fall flat. Your audience has to expect it to end one way, and the pause draws that out until you hit them with the twist ending and the deadpan delivery.

You then pause again as you wait for them to get it, then you carry on with whatever you were talking about before the joke. This second pause is very important. Then they will 'get it' and laugh. You allow yourself no more than a smile. It is not good to laugh at your own jokes. You should give them the impression that you treat it as being of no great consequence. That helps the audience to build up its own impression of you as a passably good, and hopefully very good, anecdotist or joke teller.

....

Top Tip
All jokes have an unexpected twist. That is what makes them funny.
....

Observe and listen to comedians

You may have favourite comedians that you like to watch. Do you actually observe them, though? What exactly is it about them that makes you laugh? Is it the joke or the method of telling?

In order to learn how to tell jokes yourself, watch professionals do it. Listen to their jokes and observe how they do it. Look at body language. Listen to tone, emphasis on certain words, the use (if any) of accents and accompanying mannerisms. Above all, look out for and note the pauses. They tell you a lot about their timing.

Finally, watch and listen to the punchline, the pause afterwards and then the way they carry on.

It will all be very instructive.

Mirror mirror on the wall, who is the funniest of them all?

The answer you are looking for is...you!

Back to the mirror you go and practise. This time arm yourself with some jokes and watch how you tell them. Record them as well to see how they sound. Remember you need to emphasize some words and you need to act.

Begin with a couple of the most basic jokes. The knock-knock type, the 'What do you get if you cross a ... with a ... ?' and the 'Why did the ... cross the road?' types are probably among the first jokes you heard when you were a youngster. Go to a bookshop and buy a joke book. You will find there are masses of them on the market.

This will give you the start of your material. Jot them down in your little notebook. You should already have one that is burgeoning with your small talk lines and other snippets that you have heard, observed or need to remember.

Divide your material into jokes that you could tell on different occasions. Suitable ones for the dinner table, your first date, the bar or the club, and so on. Give each section a few pages and start filling the book.

Now choose one from each section and tell it to yourself. The whole thing, and try to commit it to memory. It is patter, remember, and you want it to be slick.

Treat each joke as a mini-play. You are the actor. Act it. That means give it some expression. Use your face to tell the story. Use your body to help with appropriate gestures and signs. Be wary of accents unless you can do them well. Indeed, give a thought as to whether they are really necessary. A badly done accent is not funny and many people may regard them as offensive anyway.

Once you have made yourself laugh then try telling it to some inanimate objects. A couple of pillows, a photograph or your old teddy bear.

Then graduate to a living creature. Goldfish may not take a lot of interest, but you can focus your attention on them. Be interested in them as an audience. Gradually move up the evolutionary tree if you can. Try the cat or the dog, and when think you are ready – you may even have managed to get the dog to wag its tail – then you are ready for a person.

Top Tip

Each joke is a mini-play:
You are the actor.
You are the director.
You are playing to a live audience.

Seriously this practice on objects and on pets can help you immensely. People often do not feel comfortable telling jokes and anything that gets you focused will help. Of course, when you get to the stage of real people you are looking for a reaction. A smile will do for a start, but you really need them to laugh.

Some constructive. honest criticism may help. Depending on the relationship that you have with relatives you may get fair feedback or it could be over-critical. More often it will be polite and encouraging. Close friends may be willing to give an honest opinion.

Then at some stage, once you have learned the patter of the jokes, practised your delivery, you will be ready to start telling them.

Strategy

Somehow aim to fit at least one joke into a conversation every day. See of you can drop it into the conversation so that it fits seamlessly.

Types of jokes you may try

Apart from categorizing your jokes according to their suitability for different types of audience you can divide them up into types of joke.

BASIC JOKES

These are of the 'Knock-knock, who's there?' ilk mentioned earlier. They are just little puzzles. They can all be fitted into to casual conversations, as long as it is an appropriate point to do so. The middle of a business meeting may not be appropriate, nor would the middle of a serious chat on a first date. Drop them in when there is a lull in a conversation or if someone else has opened up a comedy moment.

ONE-LINERS

These are complete jokes in a single line (or two).

If you can come out with them at the right time they make you seem an amusing intelligent person. Or as a wag.

For example:

'My brother is a very sharp dresser; he used to cut a fine figure on the dance floor.'

PUNS

These are not usually contrived jokes. They tend to slip off the tongue. They are plays on words. If you can do them well then they can gather you a reputation as a quick wit.

Be warned, however. Once you get into the habit of them it can be a hard one to break. Then you can get the reputation for someone who tells bad jokes. Sometimes you may have to forgo the pleasure of telling one if the moment is not right.

ANECDOTAGE

Now these really can let you come into your own. An anecdote is a story about an experience that you have had. You can turn this into a joke if you act it out, embellishing it with a little exaggeration. For example:

'Then I had to offer to lift this bag for her. It was heavy. In fact, it was so heavy that I had to get the jack out of my boot to get it off the ground. Anyway, there we were in this car park, her with her shoes in her hand, hopping along on a pogo stick and me struggling with this half-ton weight of shopping.'

That clearly bears no relationship to reality and it is obvious that you are exaggerating. Yet it conjures up a comic scene which you can act out, emphasizing the heaviness, mimicking the lifting, or the old lady bouncing on a pogo stick. You give some comedic grunts and your audience are captured.

Be wary of dragging it out too long. Don't laugh as you tell it. It is a performance, remember. Build it up, add tension until you come to the end and then make sure there is some little twist that makes sense of the whole anecdote. It needs to be funny otherwise you have just told a shaggy dog story that will make the whole thing an anti-climax.

Remember, never laugh at your own jokes.

DOUBLE-ENTENDRES

These are double-meaning jokes. One meaning is logical and clean; the other is usually a bit smutty. These have to be used judiciously, since they can offend if you have misjudged your audience.

Finally just remember one thing. Even professional comedians do short gigs. Do not think that one or two well-received jokes are an invitation to do a stand-up show. Stop when you are ahead.

12

Winning arguments

There is an art to arguing.

'No, there isn't!'

You might easily imagine that the above little contradiction belongs in the last chapter on telling a joke. It could so easily be developed into a sketch, yet it could just as easily develop into a serious if futile argument.

The truth is that arguments are common. Some people love a good argument and like nothing better than to browbeat their fellows into submission. Others never argue or debate for fear of appearing foolish or uninformed. The former type is generally very confident and may be bombastic, bad tempered and belligerent. The latter tend to have confidence issues and may easily get flustered and tongue-tied, even when they know that they have a better argument.

The purpose of this chapter is to introduce you to the various strategies that can help you to win an argument.

What do we mean by argument?

Many people think of an argument as being a disagreement that is liable to end up with frayed emotions and heated tempers. In fact, many arguments do degenerate into a row like this, but some are quite calm, collected and logical.

Arguments are pretty well a normal part of life. People argue about who was first in a queue, who supports the best football team, and even whether there is or is not a god.

Arguments are put forward in philosophy, law, politics and science. Experts argue and analyse and, if one argument is accepted over all others, a conclusion is reached.

Essentially an argument is a conversation or discussion in which two or more people disagree, each putting forward a case to persuade the others to his or her point of view.

A debate is an argument carried on in front of an audience, in order to persuade the audience to accept one point or the other.

Top Tip
If you lose your temper in an argument, you have probably lost the argument.

The art of persuasion

The ancient Greeks developed the study of logic, rhetoric and sophistry. Aristotle (384–322 BC) wrote extensively about rhetoric, the art of speaking or writing effectively, and taught that to be persuasive you need to consider three things:

1 Ethos – *the character and credibility of the speaker or writer.*
2 Pathos – *the emotions of your audience.*
3 Logos – *logic and reason.*

It is a good thing to consider these three areas in relationship to any argument that you may find yourself in.

ETHOS

By this, Aristotle meant how your use of rhetoric related to your own character – that is, to your ethics and ethical standing. How trustworthy you are. This does not mean that you have to never have committed even the most minor transgression, but it implies that you have to be taking up a position that you feel comfortable with and that you think is correct. It also implies that you are going to use arguments that are true.

It also relates to anyone with whom you can align yourself who holds similar views. Thus if you can suggest that you are holding the same view and making the same argument as a noted scientist, philosopher or other expert in the relevant field, then your 'ethos' appears to be greater.

In the context of arguing in day-to-day life, I would suggest that you also extend this meaning to include the character and personality of your opponent. Make an effort to try to understand a little about your opponent because people tend to argue according to their character.

For example, at the start of this chapter I mentioned that some people browbeat their opponents into submission. I am sure that you can think of someone who adopts a bullying, hectoring attitude that brooks no discussion, and who 'wins' arguments through sheer bloody-mindedness, bad temper and bullishness.

You will also know someone who just jokes their way through an argument. They seem flippant, yet somehow get away with it and get their own way. Then there are people who get excited and enthusiastic. They natter and chatter and chip away. They may be quite repetitive and irritating.

In the old days people tried to assess individuals' characters by various means. Indeed, most people still do, according to their own way of interpreting the world and categorizing other people. Some people do it by astrological sign, others by golf handicap, style of dress, hairstyle, neatness, political persuasion, social status and so on.

There are two interesting rule of thumbs that I think are worth applying. The first is to assess how introverted or extraverted someone is. This is a measure of how outgoing they are. An extravert is liable to argue quite forcefully but not in a considered way. An introvert may shy away from argument, but may be more thoughtful when they do.

The second is to try to assess whether you have a bull, a joker or a terrier. These are not simply stereotypes – they equate with the psychologist William Sheldon's (1899–1977) concept of *somatotypes*. This was a theory he put forward linking body build with character. He came up with three types:

1 Endomorph – *the athletic sporting type; bullish and forceful.*
2 Mesomorph – *doughy, plump and jocular.*
3 Ectomorph – *slim, excitable, tenacious.*

If your opponent readily fits into one of these categories, and it is only a rule of thumb, nothing more, then you may be able to gauge what sort of argument you are going to have. Especially if you link it up with your idea of whether they are an introvert or an extravert.

PATHOS

By this Aristotle meant appealing to the emotions of the audience. If you can work out what makes them tick, the values that they hold, then you try to sway your side of the argument to appeal to them.

You may think that this means giving in to them, but it doesn't. It is just that if you can appeal to their emotions and their sense of values then you may be able to persuade them.

One of the best ways, Aristotle felt, was by anecdotes. By telling little stories. The point of narrative is that you can get people to empathize with it.

Also, use of complements can be very persuasive, rather than the scathing, insulting and spurning approach that people tend to use in argument. Rather than heaping scorn, complement them on their position, their views and values, but put your argument as something that is not all that far from theirs. Psychologically they will soften and are more likely to be persuaded.

LOGOS

This is the use of logic in the argument. Everyone thinks that they are logical in an argument, yet very often people argue from a base that is not logical. They use faulty logic or fallacies. If you can spot such a fallacy then you can bring their argument down.

Be careful, of course, about basing your own argument on a fallacy, in case someone notices. There's more on this later in the chapter.

The structure of an argument

Whether you are talking about a heated disagreement about cricket, football, politics or theology, or about an academic debate on the reality or otherwise of global warming, most arguments have the same four-layered structure.

1 Position – *your view*
   Essentially: 'I think…'
2 Proposition – *your reason for this position*
   Essentially: 'This is because…'
3 Arguments – *supporting arguments that will reinforce your proposition*
   Essentially: 'As so and so have argued…'
4 Evidence – *facts which will bear out your arguments*
   Essentially: 'This is shown by…'

It is always a good idea to have a structure on which you can base the way that you pitch in. If you have that then you are going to be working and arguing from a framework, whereas your opponent may just be winging it.

HOW TO DO IT

First of all be clear in your own mind why you are arguing:

▶ *Is it a worthwhile argument? (If not, why bother?)*
▶ *Is it a worthy argument? (Is there a principle that is worth standing up for?)*
▶ *Is it an argument that you can win? (If not, then why waste your effort?)*

If you feel that the answer to these three questions is yes, then get the four-layer structure clear in your mind. For example, if you were arguing about whether fundamentalism is logical, then you assemble your argument by looking at your position, consider your proposition and the arguments that you could bring, together with your evidence to back your statements up:

Position – *'I think that fundamentalism is naive.'*
Proposition – *'Because no area of life is so simple that you can give a fundamental rule. '*
Arguments – *'As almost every religion has fundamentalists, how can they all be right?'* *If one religion is true, how can others that are different be true?*
Or you could use this argument -'Fundamentalism flies in the face of science.'
Evidence – *'This is shown by the fact that people still believe in the Creation when evolution is a fact.'*

There are lots of views about this. People feel very emotional about it. Science has many persuasive arguments. There is a lot of evidence for scientific views, but less so for fundamentalist views, apart from religious texts written long ago.

Nevertheless people fall into three categories – believers, non-believers and agnostics. You can see how you can argue by appealing to:

Ethos – character
Pathos – emotions
Logos – reason.

You can put anything into that structure and you can see how you can present your argument. You may think it is complicated at first, but if you can think in terms of this structure, then you will be able to argue logically.

SPOT THE FALLACIES

The following are some of the fallacious arguments that people end up using:

The slippery slope
This is often used. It is also the 'thin end of the wedge' argument. It is implied that, because something is allowed, it will lead to an escalation of that something so that people will be disadvantaged.

Yet it cannot be assumed that is the case. Evidence needs to be provided in order to back it up. It is an argument that should always be challenged.

Argumentum ad verecundiam – the argument from authority
You will hear this when an authority is quoted. This can be very effective because we all tend to be in awe of authorities.

Yet an authority in one field does not mean that they are an authority in all fields. Their right of authority in the field of discussion may be legitimately challenged.

Argumentum ad hominem – the argument from the person
This is when it gets personal and an authority is discredited or
ridiculed. If someone cites an authority who has made some error,
then that may appeal to the pathos of the audience. That is, they
may take the moral high ground.

Argumentum ad antiquitatem – the argument from tradition
You will recognize this when someone argues that it is as it is
because it has always been done this way.

Yet – new ways may be more effective.

Argumentum ad ignorantiam – the argument from ignorance
This is when it is assumed that something is true just because it
has not been proven to be false. You could say that all religions are
based on such an argument.

Argumentum ad logicam – the argument from logic
This is when something is assumed to be false just because
a supporting theory has been disproved or discredited.
Complementary medicine may be rubbished in an argument
because it does not conform to known scientific fact.

However, science does not hold all the answers because not
everything is known. There may be as yet undiscovered scientific
principles at work that would legitimize it.

Dicto simpliciter – the sweeping generalization
It should be easy to puncture this and let the wind out. Don't
accept that *all* scientists believe such and such, or that *any* rational
person will think so and so.

Argumentum ad misericordiam – the argument from mercy
This is when one party makes a statement which will arouse
feelings of pity or humanity in the other party, so that they cannot
argue against for fear of seeming cruel or pitiless. This is a decided
appeal to pathos.

Argumentum ad nauseam – the argument to the point of nausea
Here repetition is used until the opponent gives up in exasperation.
It is a bullying approach, that I mentioned at the beginning of the
chapter. When it is used the person often gets louder and louder,
but without adding any logic to the process.

This has to be challenged and the person asked to produce facts in
support of their argument, otherwise it is invalidated.

Argumentum ad numerum – the argument from numbers
Beware of this when statistics are brought in. Quite simply,
statistics can be distorted in favour or against. Sixty per cent for
something means 40 per cent against, which is not insignificant. A
'majority' may mean only 51 per cent.

Understand the bias of statistics and do not just accept them at face
value. Numbers persuade people by appealing to ethos (by virtue
of the researchers), by pathos (by virtue of the emotions of the
audience) and by logos (because mathematics and statistics seem
totally reasonable).

Non sequitur
This means that an argument doesn't follow. Someone may believe
that they are being logical and that they are providing evidence for
their case, but they may in fact have missed out a stage or two in
reasoning. Often you will hear people use the words 'so' or 'therefore'.

'Too much sugar has been shown to cause dental caries, so you
shouldn't eat sweets.'

'Why not? You can always brush your teeth. You don't have to eat
all that many sweets.'

Taken to its extreme you can call it a quantum leap argument.

Politician's answer
You can spot this when people take a long time to answer. They
go round the houses and answer the question they want to answer,

only coming to the point at the end of their mini-speech when they have had time to think. It is as if they have gone on to autopilot in the meanwhile.

Strategy for a good argument

▶ *Understand the structure of an argument – position, proposition, arguments, evidence.*
▶ *Understand the way of appealing to your opponent or audience – ethos, pathos, logos.*
▶ *Try to assess your opponent's character as an introvert or extravert and according to Sheldon's somatotypes.*
▶ *Be calm – do not lose your temper. If you lose it you will lose the argument.*
▶ *Try to be factual. Use real facts and statistics.*
▶ *Spot fallacious arguments. Try to be logical yourself.*
▶ *Be a good listener. Show your opponent that you are listening to their argument and not just overriding them or attempting to sweep their argument aside.*
▶ *Be sporting and accept good points. Complement your opponent on good points made.*
▶ *Be ready with a counter-argument.*
▶ *Use persuader words. These are words like 'surely', 'truly', 'clearly' and 'obviously'.*

13

Presentations

Break a leg!

The actor's maxim

Mention the word 'presentation' to most students, whether they are 16 or 26 and a large number will cringe. The thought of getting up before your peers and exposing your work and style of performing is often enough to set the heart racing and cause the sweat glands to pump out beads of perspiration on the brow and cause an uncomfortable moistness under the arms. We are of course back to that age-old fear of public speaking. It does not matter whether the person has a burning ambition to be a lawyer or a politician; most people dislike all attention being focused on them.

Anticipatory anxiety is the problem, but as you will realize if you have read straight through the book, it can be dealt with by using the various strategies in the book. If you have come straight to this chapter I recommend that you go back and read through Chapter 1 and the strategies that I have discussed there.

Don't compare yourself with others

Most people when they are faced with giving a presentation for the very first time imagine that they will be awful at it and that they will never be as good as their friends or their peers. It doesn't matter whether you have never heard your friend giving a presentation or not, it is likely that your inner critic will conjure up another of the 'what if' scenarios:

'What if my trousers fall down?'
'What if my flies are undone?'
'What if I can't get a word out?'
'What if they all think I am such a fool?'

Do those sound familiar? It is not surprising if they do because they are common complaints. Yet none of them are likely. They are all just typical examples of the way that the inner critic gets you into a fluster beforehand. He doesn't want you to make a fool of yourself, so he keeps on telling you about all the things that can go wrong, so that you can avoid them. It doesn't work that way, of course, because the very act of trying not to think about these things will make you focus on them.

Why do you think actors tell each other to break a leg before they begin a performance? A bit of superstition, of course, but it is quite a good piece of advice. If you worry about stumbling and injuring yourself, then you introduce tension – you focus so hard on not doing something that you are then liable to stumble and injure yourself...and possibly even break a leg! Telling you to do something, on the other hand, will have the opposite effect. It seems banal and the whole business is then quickly forgotten.

It is a good example of paradoxical intention, one of the techniques that I mentioned in Chapter 1 in the section on Viktor Frankl and logotherapy.

Strategy

Giving a presentation is giving a performance. Remember before you go – break a leg!

But if you do compare yourself with others ...

Then don't worry. The simple truth is that no one ever does as well as they want. Indeed, most people are only ever pretty good. Actors and politicians may give excellent performances, but ordinary lecturers, teachers, and other professionals only ever do all right.

That might sound very negative and a bit derogatory about respected members of a highly respected profession. Yet how many of them ever inspire you? How much of their lessons or lectures do you remember? How much of anyone's speech do you recall?

The answer is that at best you will remember about a third. The rest of the time your mind will be wandering. You may find yourself thinking ahead to something you want to do or somewhere you plan to go. You may focus on someone or on several people in the room or hall who appeal to you. You may even just go into a little trance, a little daydream, so that you suddenly come back to the speaker realizing that you did not catch their last utterance.

The interesting thing is that there are a lot of people who love the sound of their own voice and will gladly get up to speak, and then bore everyone to tears.

You are not going to do that. You are going to give a good performance, possibly even a very good performance, as long as you do one thing.

You practise.

Top Tip
You do not have to be word perfect.

Know your subject

This is fundamental, of course. If you are called upon to make a presentation then the last thing you ever do is to do it without being prepared. Would you expect a surgeon to begin an operation without knowing precisely what he was going to do? He or she would not go into the operating theatre with a textbook to refer to as he or she went along.

A Formula 1 driver would never set off in a race without knowing all about the racetrack.

A conductor would not get onto the rostrum without knowing the music he was going to conduct.

Do I need to go further?

Prepare your subject

This is also fundamental, yet it is amazing how often people do not do this. It happens a lot in business, and in professions like medicine. Although someone may have an intimate and even expert knowledge of their subject, it does not mean that they can just get up and spout out words of wisdom. If you are not prepared, it does not matter whether you are the most laid-back person on the planet, you will not give the performance of which you are capable. It will not come off as well as you hoped and your listeners, whether they are employees, colleagues, students or clients, will be less impressed than you wanted them to be.

Do not ever allow yourself to fall into sloppy thinking and excuse yourself by saying you did not have time to prepare. Of course you have time! It is all a question of priorities. If you want to give a good presentation then take the time and prepare properly.

WHAT YOU NEED TO PREPARE

Well, the first thing is the topic that you are going to present. Let us imagine having a chat with three people in advance of their different types of presentation.

Person 1

So what are you going to talk to the Women's Institute about?
Budgerigars.

OK, presumably you know a lot about them?
I keep them as a hobby.

That's a start. I expect you must be an expert. Have you done some research?
No, I just like them and look after them.

I see. So how do you plan to present your presentation? I assume that you are going to prepare a talk, not just get up there and (excuse the pun) wing it.
Ha! That's good, a joke. Well, I might put a joke or two in. People like jokes.

Have you got a plan for the talk?
I might jot down some ideas beforehand.

Are you going to use any visual aids?
I have some photos I thought I could hand round.

You can imagine how much fun that talk is going to be, can't you? What about this one?

Person 2

What is the title of your evening class lecture?
The Russian Revolution.

Wow! That's a big topic. What are you going to focus on?
The whole thing. I'm going to rattle through it. I've been fascinated by it all my life.

Have you prepared it well?
I've written detailed notes. I should be able to get through it if I talk fast. I read quickly.

Are you using visual aids?
No. I hate them. Just a straight lecture.

That could be scintillating, but how many people will be awake for a whole read-out lecture, do you think?

How about this?

Person 3

What is your presentation to your chemistry class about?
It's about the Periodic Table of the Elements.

Are you interested in that?
Not really. I just have to do it. I'm really scared about it. There are some eggheads in the class and they might show me up.

How are you going to cope with the nerves?
No idea. Just hope they go away.

Are you well prepared? Have you made notes?
No notes. I've just done a PowerPoint and have lots of jazzy effects with pictures zooming in and words materializing.'

Have you practised it?
No way. I don't like to think about it, really. I may run through it the night before.

Although these three conversations are imagined, they are not far from the way that people prepare for talks and presentations. That is to say that people do not really know what they should prepare. They do not plan properly, they do not think about a focus for their talk and they do not rehearse.

They should do all of those.

Good planning

Let's break this down into:

▶ *planning the talk*
▶ *rehearsing your performance.*

PLANNING THE TALK

Focus
First take your topic and think about the focus. That doesn't just mean thinking of the title, although that is important. I would liken this to thinking up and writing a story. Let me explain.

When I start the process of writing a novel I usually begin with a character. He or she is my focus. The story is going to be about that person. Then comes the theme, what the story is about. For example, I wrote a crime novel set on the Outer Hebridean island of West Uist. Don't go looking for an atlas; you won't find it because it is fictitious. I had my main character as the focus and I developed a story idea, a theme about him. Before I could go further I had to get a title in my mind. It doesn't matter whether it was going to be the finished title for when the novel was completed, but it had to fit the story and the theme. The novel was called *The Gathering Murders* and it was a detective story set during a literary festival and Highland gathering. Once I had those elements set in my mind I was able to craft the novel.

This is exactly the same when you start planning a talk or presentation. You need to think of the topic, the focus, the theme and the title.

Let us take the above example about budgerigars. That is the topic and it is also the presenter's choice of title. That is OK as long as he has thought out a focus for the talk and a theme. I suspect he hadn't.

The talk would have more chance of being memorable if he focused on one aspect about budgerigars. I know nothing about them myself, but suppose he decided to focus on himself as a pet-owner. The theme could be about how a pet-owner goes about looking after his budgerigars. The title could be more specific as a result. Perhaps: '*Teach your budgerigar to love life.*'

That is not intended to be flippant. It says something about the speaker. He wants to impart a message. There is a theme to the talk and there is a promise that you will come away having learned something from his enthusiastic talk.

Structure

Next comes structure. You need to sketch out the structure of your talk. That does not mean that you just make detailed notes. You need to assemble the things that you are going to include. A lot of people think that means that they need to include everything they can about the subject. They cram in as many facts as possible.

Unless you are giving a didactic lecture that people are going to scribble notes on, or record for reference later, that is not a good idea! Your audience will not take everything in. Information overload stops people from concentrating. The brain finds it too difficult and the mind will wander.

If you want to impart important information, then just give the salient information. Perhaps only give a handful of main points and build on them. Once you go beyond that people will not retain the information. This includes all types of audience. It is not an indictment of their intelligence; it is just a fact.

I have written a newspaper column for almost three decades. When I started I was so keen to get all the information that I could about a subject that I would write and rewrite until I had it word perfect. I think those early articles were tolerably good. At any rate I am still writing the column. Now, however, I write far more succinctly and, I am told, more interestingly. The thing is that people will only recall about three facts in an article. That doesn't matter whether it is a huge whole-page article or a column of 350 words. I therefore only include three or four facts.

That may not cheer you up if you are preparing a major talk, but if you want to impress people with your talk the first thing to do is give them three or four, half a dozen at the most, memorable pieces of information.

Top Tip

Less is more when you are giving a talk. The majority of people do not retain more than three or four pieces of information from a lecture.

The next very important thing is to reinforce those pieces of information by repetition. You may have thought that you are going to rattle through everything, covering all the main points just once. Think again.

Suppose you have one single burning aim in mind. You may have developed a new way of training a budgerigar to talk or sing. It may be quite a complex process, yet the kernel of the method may be quite succinct. If you want people to take up your method, then repeat that kernel three times in the lecture. Find different ways of actually saying it, but give the message three times.

If you listen to a politician talking you will see that they use repetition of key points that they want to emphasize and get across to their audience. If you really want to research this then look out the speeches of great orators like Winston Churchill, J.F. Kennedy and Martin Luther King.

> ## Top Tip
> A message that is repeated during a talk will be reinforced and is more likely to be remembered by a listener.

The structure of your talk should also be logical. First of all, how long have you been allocated? Is there any flexibility in that? Is there going to be time for questions after your talk or will you have to allocate time within your time slot? These are things you need to know in advance.

Once you know long you have, you can build the talk accordingly. You may have been given a whole hour, which is a long time to talk for. You may think you need that long, but really you are not likely to. Remember that less is more. You can give a really good talk in half or three-quarters of the time and have time for interaction afterwards. That is often the most useful part, since you have given the information you want to give, so you are basically in control of the questions that will come from it.

A beginning, middle and end
Don't just choose a topic and rattle through it. You have already worked out focus, theme and title. Now give it a beginning, middle and an end, just as you want to see in a story or a film. I will come to the performance of the talk in due course, but for now we are talking about content and the way that you are going to fit that into the talk.

The *beginning* introduces the topic of the talk to the audience and you lead them into the subject. It has to be interesting and you have to show your enthusiasm for the subject.

The *middle* is the time that people may drift off into daydreams or sleep; indeed, they may even get up and wander off if you haven't grabbed their interest. If that happens by the way, don't let it phase you. Just assume that they have to leave early to go and catch a bus, or make another appointment. Never take it personally.

You do have to retain their interest, however, so you have to have some way of doing that. Visual aids are one way, but don't overdo them.

Another very positive way is by telling a story. It has to be relevant, of course, so make it an anecdote that ties up with or which naturally arises from the topic in hand. Stories provide talks with a narrative hook. People actually retain things better if you give them some information in story format. They really do. If you can instil some humour into it that is great. If humour is not appropriate, then consider using some drama.

The middle is a good time to use that repetition I was talking about. You can do it by using lines like this:

'Let me bring you back to...'
'Here is an example of how it might look if...'
'OK, so let me remind you about...'
'So let us look at how this can translate into....'

Raymond Chandler, the crime writer and screenwriter, used to advise that, when things start to get dull, you should bring in a man with a gun. That means introduce the unexpected, something that will grab attention. You might need to use a gimmick, something that will wake them up and get them listening again.

If we go back to our student who was going to talk about the Periodic Table, this might be a point to do an experiment – as long as you don't cause an explosion or breach health and safety regulations.

Then you approach the *end*. Get ready for more repetition to reinforce the message. You will have given the bulk of your talk and this part is about drawing it all together. It needs to be satisfying like a good book or film. People will sense that you are coming to the end, and they will have shaken off the mid-talk lethargy. They will be more receptive to information again.

Give yourself enough time to summarize your points and to draw your conclusion. The actual end should be a bit like a cliff-hanger, leaving them wanting more.

Then the questions.

Then the applause and a crisp exit from the limelight.

Strategy

STRATEGY

Plan your talk. This is more than just writing an essay to regurgitate. It is a script for a play that you are going to act out. All of the following areas need attending to:

▶ *Choosing the topic*
▶ *Selecting a focus*
▶ *Choosing a theme*
▶ *Getting the title right*
▶ *Timing*
▶ *Working out the structure – beginning, middle and end*
▶ *Focusing on the points to be made and when to repeat them*
▶ *Using an anecdote, gimmick, the 'man with a gun' in the middle*
▶ *Using a succinct summary and a crisp close*
▶ *Leaving time for questions.*

REHEARSING YOUR PERFORMANCE

This may sound more than you had bargained for, but if you want to dazzle your audience and give a skilful and memorable presentation then you need to treat it in the right manner. That means that you need to practise so that you appear crisp, polished and confident.

Before you pitch in there are certain things that you need to know. This is all part of the preparation and it is all an important part of the rehearsal process. You need to know about:

▶ *your audience*
▶ *the venue*
▶ *what facilities you will have.*

Audience

You might not have given it much thought, other than to start thinking about the whole thing with trepidation. You shouldn't do that. You need to get into the right mindset. This is your opportunity to shine in the limelight. Other people would give their eye-teeth to be doing it, so look forward with eager anticipation not anticipatory fear. Go back to Chapter 1 and go through the strategies I outlined there.

Do you know any of the people who will be in the audience? That can be helpful, since friendly faces always help. If you don't, then that is also a bonus, since there is nothing to fear from them.

Is it a professional audience, a peer group audience or is it a mixture of all types, as you might expect at any paying event?

How many people are likely to be in the audience?

Top Tip

An audience is just a collection of individuals. It does not have a collective intelligence like a swarm of bees or a flock of birds. Although it may be a large audience, it is not a large 'creature'; it is just a group of people. No need for fear.

The venue

It is good to know if you are going to be talking on a platform or dais. Whether you will have a seat, a desk, a table or a lectern. Will the audience be seated lecture-fashion or will they be in groups, at individual tables, on settees, easy chairs, or even standing? What are the acoustics like?

Facilities

Is there a sound system? Visual aids equipment? Is there going to be anyone present who can handle technology if needed? Will your audiovisual aids be compatible?

Knowing about all of these factors helps you to prepare for your performance. Like an actor you can adapt your performance according to the audience, venue and facilities. You accommodate it all into your imagined environment as you rehearse.

Script and rehearsal

You do this in a room with a full-length mirror. Have your notes ready and a clock to time yourself according to how much time you have been allowed. Dress as you will be dressed, because that helps to reinforce the realism of the talk in your mind. Do whichever strategy you find best to relax you beforehand.

Choose which sort of tone is going to be right for this audience. Refresh your memory and look at this in Chapter 5, 'Appreciate your voice'.

You do not actually have to set the structure out as you would write down the words of a play in detail, but do draft it out in note form so that you can refer to this. You can either incorporate this into your presentation notes, or have a separate sheet or card that you can refer to alongside. You may even just want to do it in a visual flow chart. If you are a visual (check your NLP representational system type in Chapter 6), then you may find this the best way.

First deal with the opening. This starts from the moment you are introduced, so you will need to start rehearsing from that point. You get up and walk to the podium, speaker's point or whatever is arranged. Do this in your imagination and walk to the mirror.

Do not say anything until you are in position; just look (or act) confident. Before you say a word give a big smile, as if you are happy to have been introduced and you are happy to be doing this talk. As you do this, look around the room (or the hall in your mind) and engage four or five people with eye contact.

Now you say thank you to the host, master of ceremonies or chairperson in a clear voice.

Then it is time to recite a piece of the patter we talked about and for which you wrote a piece in Chapter 5. It should be well practised – knowing precisely what to say will get you off to a good start. When you are in the midst of the real talk or lecture, this is not the time to fumble for words to get you off the starting blocks.

I have a habit of doing a magic trick at the start of lectures. Not straight away but after I have given my patter, which usually gives me an excuse to pick up a prop of some sort. The audience do not know that it is a magic prop; it is perhaps a book or some seemingly everyday object. I use misdirection here, the basis of all conjuring tricks, to make the audience think they are seeing one thing, then something totally different is seen.

This is an attention grabber. It usually works for me and since I like to do conjuring tricks it gets me into the right mindset. The patter has already been practised so I have selected the tone that is going to be right for the audience. The thing that you must do if you use a trick or gimmick at the start, of course, is to maintain that interest all the way through the talk.

The format of the venue needs to be taken into account. If you are on a platform then you just imagine that. If you are in a round-robin sort of situation, then you can move around, but be careful of bobbing around too much. It may be better to just turn so that you are interacting with everyone at some stage. Use eye contact all the time.

About five or ten minutes into the talk you should have planted the first of the main points that you want them to take away. You then elucidate and elaborate from that point for ten minutes, then bring up the next main point.

About halfway through, get ready to do something attention-grabbing. Use a gimmick, tell a joke or give them an anecdote. And follow up with a repetition of a salient point.

By now you should be sailing merrily along. Don't lose them. Keep them with you. Use your voice to emphasize certain important points. And use body language, too. Remember that you are a performer and you want them to like your performance. Your task is not just to get up, spout and then sit down again. You are there to do the best job that you can and make it an experience that they will remember favourably.

Move into the final part, remembering to repeat main points. Then you arrive at the summary. Actually tell them that this is happening. Then make a conclusion and then go straight into thanking them. Say that you have enjoyed talking to them and ask if they have any questions.

That is how you do it. You run through the whole thing, and you practise it again on at least another occasion – I would suggest at least three times in advance of the talk. You will find that you improve each time. You will also find that you are more relaxed each time you do it.

When you actually come to do it you will capitalize on those rehearsals. Don't have any quibbles about practising. That is what actors, professional speakers and politicians do. If it is good enough for them it is good enough for you.

Don't overload your audience with statistics that they cannot possibly recall. Keep it simple. You must always be able to defend statistics that you use.

Body language

As you are well aware from earlier chapters of this book, body language is incredibly important when you get up to talk and present. The main thing is to appear confident. Practising in the mirror will help you to groom that confident look. You have to try to look natural and relaxed and enthusiastic about your subject. If you are not really interested in the subject then act as though you are. For the purposes of the talk it is your passion.

Eye contact is the best thing you can do. The second is to use your face expressively. You will have been regularly trying out the exercises we covered in Chapter 7. So be expressive and smile a lot. You will have practised the right type of smiles which will be appropriate for the talk and the setting of the talk.

Above all, keep your hands away from your face and head. Do not stroke your chin or cheek. Do not scratch your head, unless it is a deliberate pantomimic gesture to indicate puzzlement.

Make body movements appropriate. If you are standing there in character as a professor, then behave like one. Don't have any inappropriate body swaying, rotations or seesaw movements. These all just look nervous. Adopt a calm, well-rooted posture – remember you are playing the part of the expert on this subject.

Use your hands well. This does not mean that you wave them about like a conductor. Hand movements should have a definite purpose, not resemble a budgerigar flapping its wings. Keep them apart and avoid wringing them, rubbing them together or holding them.

Confident people do not need to guard themselves and they keep unnecessary movements to a minimum.

Showing the palms is a good thing. It shows that you are open and friendly. People are attracted to this gesture. Try it out in front of the mirror; be open-handed in your rehearsals. Think, talk and watch your hands.

When you are making your salient points you can use your hands for emphasis. Remember to aim at only a few main points. Suppose you are going to discuss five main things in the whole talk. You can indicate point one by raising your left open hand and touch the thumb with your right hand. When you come to point two, do the same but touch your index finger, and so on. This will tend to register with the audience. Then when you summarize, take them back to the points and repeat.

Visual aids

Many people hide behind their visual aids. PowerPoint has placed an incredible array of effects in the hands of anyone who has access to a computer. 'Death by PowerPoint' is now a common term bandied around, meaning that the message that one is trying to convey gets lost in a storm of special effects. I know this only too well – I admit to having been guilty of it myself in the past. Here are a few pointers:

- ▶ *The old Chinese expression 'a picture paints a thousand words' is true. Regard it as such and any visual that you use should save you some wordage, because you don't have to spend the time describing what you have just shown.*
- ▶ *Visual aids should simply mean that one is using a visual to aid the transmission of information. It must not be regarded as a replacement.*

▶ Do not make the mistake of flashing up a series of bullet points, and then read them off the screen. Why would you do that? The audience can read and they can hear. They don't want to read while they listen to you reading the same thing.

▶ You should not really need to look up at them, because you have them in front of you on the computer. The audience do not really want to see your back or the back of your head.

▶ The downside of using visual aids is that, while the visual is up, the attention is off you. That is not what you want to happen, whatever you may think. When you are up there talking you want the audience to be with you, following you, not focusing on a screen with you standing in the shadows. Remember that your body language is a main part of the show. Turning your back on the audience is negative body language.

Strategy

Plan the talk.
Rehearse beforehand.

14

Making a speech

Most people can expect to be asked to make a speech at some time or another. It may be a happy occasion, like a wedding, a celebration or a dinner. It may be just a few words off the cuff or something that people expect to be entertained by, like a best man's speech or an after-dinner speech. Or it may be something altogether more sombre, like a funeral oration.

These are all very different types of speech, but you are capable of making any one of them. As with most types of talking, although being asked to make a speech may alarm you as a prospect, you can do it as long as you are prepared, you have strategies to help you and you have practised.

There is a great difference between giving a lecture or doing a talk and making a speech. It is all to do with time. Whereas a talk or a lecture presentation will have a definite time, because you have been given a slot and you have to use it to the best of your ability, a speech can be a lot shorter. Indeed, it *should* be much shorter; otherwise you will bore everyone.

I am sure that you will have heard of President Abraham Lincoln's Gettysburg Address. This is one of the most famous American speeches of all time. It was delivered at the dedication of the Soldiers' National Cemetery in Gettysburg in 1863, during the American Civil War. In it Lincoln began with the words:

'Four score and seven years ago...'

This referred to the Declaration of Independence of 1776. He then went on to talk about the principles of equality and the rights of all people. He said that the ceremony gave them an opportunity to not only dedicate the cemetery to the fallen, but to consecrate the living in their endeavour to ensure that they won:

'... and that government of the people, by the people, for the people, shall not perish from the earth.'

Those are immortal lines. They forged a national spirit. Yet the whole speech only took two minutes.

Top Tip
A speech should be shorter than a lecture or a prepared talk.

Could you just say a few words?

Before we talk about the different types of speech that you will have time to go and prepare and practise for, let us talk about the sort that tends to fill people with horror. The type that is suddenly dropped on you at an event for some reason or another. Perhaps someone is ill, or someone is leaving a job or position, and you are felt to be the most appropriate person to say a few words off the cuff.

There should not really be any reason to get anxious about this. You should be flattered to be asked. Besides, although you might not have been expecting it, you can still practise for such occasions! Just have a strategy in hand.

An example

'Joan has been with us for twenty-five years and she's retiring today.'

Now if you are being asked to say a few words at her retirement lunch you can easily cobble together an impressive little impromptu speech. You either know, or can quickly find out:

▶ *Joan's full name*
▶ *her job*
▶ *what the job entailed*
▶ *how long she has been with the organization*
▶ *her special way of doing whatever her job was*
▶ *her outside interests*
▶ *her family*
▶ *her sense of humour.*

Armed with those you can construct a few little lines that will not take long. Something like this:

'Could I just have a few minutes of your time? We are here together on this special day to celebrate Joan Banting's retirement.'

(Smile at Joan and smile at the audience.)

'Believe it or not, but Joan has been with us for twenty-five years. That's five years longer than me. In fact, I remember when I came to the organization...'

(Time for a short anecdote if you can recall that first meeting.)

'She helped me then as I was finding my feet, and she has kept on helping. Whenever anyone has needed help with...'

(A little about her job.)

'And she always had her own way of doing things...'

(Give an example of how she did her examinations, typing, interviewing or whatever.)

'Her work over the years has helped to keep the wheels of the organization rolling on with slick efficiency, but now she is hanging up her...'

[Stethoscope, lab coat, etc.]

'...so that she can spend more time with...'

[Names of family and relations.]

'...and indulge her passion for...'

[Golf, wood-turning, writing, travel, etc.]

'I am going to really miss her and just want to ask her to keep in touch.'

[Smile at Joan again and touch her hand perhaps if appropriate.]

'Joan, we are all going to miss you and as a token of all of our esteem we have a gift for you...'

Not difficult was it? And so with a little strategy you can always do an off-the-cuff for someone leaving.

Strategy

For an off-the-cuff speech for someone at work or associated with a club or society remember this little mnemonic PRAY FOR ME:

Person – who it is about
Role – their role
About them and the way they performed that role
Years that they have completed
Family – partner, spouse, children, etc

Outside interests
Reason for going, the ceremony, etc
Me – what your relationship has been to the person
Emotion – that you feel about this occasion

Wedding speeches

Weddings are supposed to be among the happiest days of people's lives. Two people tie the knot, take vows and promise themselves to each other for life eternal. That is the traditional view. Nowadays it may be simply until the expiry of the contract at a time agreed by both parties' lawyers.

That is not meant to be flippant; it is simply a statement of fact, since in the UK divorce has been getting increasingly common and as a result people often have multiple wedding ceremonies and some even have divorce parties. What on earth, you may wonder, does one say at a divorce party?

We will come to that, since to dwell on it is definitely a case of putting the cart before the horse. So to start, I am going to assume that this wedding is between two people ecstatically in love who cannot foresee ever being apart. That is how I would like to view marriage and it is my hope that the wedding you are preparing for is made in heaven and will last for ever.

Top Tip
No need to worry, because everyone is behind all of the speakers at a wedding.

TRADITIONAL WEDDING ETIQUETTE

There is a set order in which the speeches at a wedding are made. You can, of course, do things however you want if it is your wedding, but the following is the traditional format.

People often feel anxious before wedding speeches, whichever part they are playing in it, yet there is no need. Weddings are occasions when absolutely everyone is there to make it the best possible day that they can for the bride and groom, so everyone is behind the speakers and they will laugh and clap spontaneously.

Many people have a master of ceremonies who will gain the attention of the guests and introduce the different speakers. If there is no master of ceremonies then the first speaker begins.

Father of the bride

The reason that the bride's father begins is simply because in days gone by (if not still now) he paid for the whole thing so was entitled to welcome everyone.

The father of the bride is not expected to ramble on interminably or to crack sarcastic jokes. He speaks with some authority and should be dignified as the head of his family. He is giving his daughter away to someone that he clearly respects and feels happy to entrust his beloved daughter to.

There are seven parts to the father of the bride's speech:

1 *On behalf of your wife and yourself, welcome everyone to the wedding. Welcome especially to the family of the groom. Comment perhaps on how well and happy they look. You hope and assume that they are feeling as happy as you are on this joyous occasion.*
2 *Draw attention to your daughter and tell everyone how beautiful and radiant she looks today. Tell everyone that it is one of the most momentous days of your life to walk your daughter down the aisle (if it was a church wedding). Say how proud you are of her, of her achievements, her kindness and her nature.*
3 *Here you can be a little bit witty and tell an anecdote or two – no more – about her as a child or teenager. Nothing too embarrassing, of course, since the father of the bride is the last person who wants to ruin her special day.*

4 *Welcome the groom into the family. Recount your first
   meeting and tell the guests that you could see how well suited
   you knew the two of them were. Perhaps a light-hearted
   anecdote, but nothing embarrassing here either. It is the job of
   the best man to do that!*
5 *You should offer some advice about married life, based on
   your own experience. Perhaps talk about golf, or football, or
   some shared interest you have with the groom.*
6 *Thank everyone who has helped to make this a special day.
   The vicar, priest or registrar. The caterers. Anyone special who
   has come from far.*
7 *Propose a toast to the bride and groom.*

There may be variants to this that you choose to make.
Circumstances may mean that there is no father of the bride, in
which case another relative, or even the mother of the bride, may
choose to speak. That is fine; the principles of the speech are just
the same.

The MC then introduces the groom. If you do not have one, then
the father of the bride makes the introduction.

The groom
This speech is not expected to be funny, apart from telling a little
joke at the start. It is the speech of a loving man who is about to
spend the rest of his life with the love of his life. He is respectful to
her family and appreciative of the fact that he is being welcomed
into the family today:

There are six parts to his speech.

1 *Begin with a simple joke. Everyone will laugh and it will get
   rid of any nerves. 'On behalf of my wife and me.' Simply that!
   It is the first time you have said it, and it will sound strange
   and a little funny. It always works. There are other jokes
   that you can fish out on the Internet, if you wish, but this old
   chestnut is still a great starter.*

2 You thank the bride's parents for having raised such a
   wonderful daughter. She is a credit to them, whom you plan to
   cherish and look after for the rest of your life.

3 You tell everyone how happy you are to be standing here
   today, having married your bride. Complement her on her
   qualities, her beauty and her charm. Time for an anecdote
   about your first meeting, your courtship and the moment she
   agreed to be your wife.

4 Thank everyone who has helped to make this day so special.
   The caterers, the guests, the vicar, etc.

5 Thank the bridesmaids or matron of honour and propose a
   toast to them.

6 Say that you want to thank your best man, but you stand in
   some trepidation about some of the things that he may be
   about to reveal. Make a little joke about having paid him for
   his silence, perhaps.

The MC introduces the best man, but if there is no MC the groom
does so.

The best man

This is the speech that everyone has been waiting for. This is the
speech that everyone expects to hear a few jokes told at the expense
of the groom, and possibly one or two at the expense of the bride
(although the latter should only ever be light, whimsical jokes).

There are six main parts to the best man's speech:

1 Thank the groom for inviting you to be the best man here on
   this special day. Thank also both families.

2 Tell the guests how you and the groom met. It is best to
   do this straight to begin with, and then tell a joke. For
   example, 'All of that led me to believe that ... was the most
   straightforward and upstanding of fellows. Little did I suspect
   that there would be a darker side!'

3 Then straight into the anecdotes about the groom. Three or
   four will do. Too many and you risk boring people.

4   A *few words about the bride. You may say something like, 'and then he met ... and we knew that something incredible had happened. How exactly did someone as beautiful as ... fall in love with someone as – well – ordinary as (the groom).' Deliver an anecdote or two (at the most) about the bride's effect on the groom.*

5   *Now read a few cards that have been sent. Better actually to read a selection and indicate that you will display them on the table with the wedding presents for the guests to see later on. Choose a couple from the senior members of the families and a couple of funny (but not salacious) ones.*

6   *Toast your friends, the bride and groom again.*

The bride
Nowadays the bride may choose to say a few words herself. There is no set content for the bride, but it will tend to mirror that of the groom. A lot of newly-weds choose this moment to perform their first married duty by giving gifts to the bridesmaids or matron of honour and the best man.

Strategy

At the next wedding you go to, pay very close attention to the speeches. Tick off all the points that have been covered in the individual speeches. Time each one as well and see which you found to be satisfying, which too long, and which started to make people yawn.

Divorce speeches

As I mentioned at the start of wedding speeches, divorce is far more common these days than it was 50 years ago.

People whose marriage comes to an end often feel depressed that they have failed in their marriage. They may feel isolated from family that they knew well and they get a feeling that no one can understand what they have gone through or feel the pain that they have had. Other people may feel relieved and happy that they have ended a relationship that did not flourish.

It has to be said, however, that divorce is never truly a happy state. The two people obviously had feelings for one another and they presumably must have had some happy times together.

A few statistics

- ▶ *Seventy per cent of divorces are first marriages.*
- ▶ *Most divorces occur in the first two years.*
- ▶ *Half of divorcing couples have at least one child under the age of 16 years.*
- ▶ *The average age at divorce for a man is 42 and for a woman it is 39 years.*

People do hold divorce parties (usually for just one of the spouses and not two!) and many do want to get things off their chest with a speech. It is hard for many to speak fondly or kindly of their former spouse. The speech may be a means of getting rid of some of the pent-up emotions that have built up from the end of the marriage and through the divorce period. This is more often the case if it has been especially acrimonious.

So, what do you want to say at the divorce speech? You need to ask yourself a lot of questions:

- ▶ *What is the purpose of my speech?*
- ▶ *Whom am I trying to impress?*
- ▶ *Whom am I trying to shock?*
- ▶ *Is this speech for me?*
- ▶ *Who is going to be there? Family, friends, work colleagues?*

- *Are you going to have mutual friends who will report back?*
- *Is it a celebration of the fact that you have parted?*
- *Is it a victory speech?*
- *Do you want it to be a cathartic speech to let out all the pent-up aggravation caused by the divorce?*

Analyse all of that and decide what you really want. You may make a lot of people uncomfortable. Your family may feel relieved. Your children, if they are present and old enough to understand, may be traumatised even more. Mutual friends will not know how to react.

Keep it short. That is the first thing to ensure. If Abraham Lincoln could make one of the greatest speeches in two minutes, that is plenty of time for you.

Dignity is the best approach. While getting up and having a rant may make you feel better, the truth is that it will not do anything for your image. A controlled and dignified announcement that the marriage is over and that you have finally parted is what most people want to hear, not a diatribe about how awful the other person was.

It is good to be as magnanimous as you are able to be. People will respect you as a person for that. Acknowledge that you did have good times. If there are children indicate that they are the living proof of that.

Be philosophical. Life is never simple or predictable. The events that led up to the divorce happened and they cannot be undone. You are not the first person to be divorced and you will not be the last.

You accept that life moves on and that now you have the opportunity for a new beginning.

You thank your friends and relatives for their support.

Then you finish.

Funeral oration

Some of the greatest speeches ever made have been funeral orations – a person's life immortalized in the course of a few minutes.

Every life deserves some words of respect and if you are called to talk about a deceased relative, friend or colleague, you should accept and do your best to celebrate their life. Always try to remember that no matter how the deceased person died, you have to celebrate the time on Earth that they shared with others, and draw out all the positive effects that their life had on others.

It is also worth appreciating that a funeral speech will actually help in the grieving process.

COLLECT YOUR INFORMATION

You are going to have time before the funeral to collect your information. Ask the relatives who knew the deceased best for their best memories. They can just be jotted down and reassembled into a chronological sequence later on. Build up a picture.

Have a look at old photographs, home videos and scrapbooks. Find out about their home life, their interests and their work.

MAKE A BRIEF FRAMEWORK

Having gathered your information jot it down into a set order. Include the following, as appropriate:

▶ *Mention the person's full name at the start, then refer to them by their first name. Mention where they were born, when and where they spent their life latterly. Whom they were related to and when they died. (Decide with the family as to whether or not the cause of death is to be mentioned.)*

▶ *Early life – include a few anecdotes that you have been given to emphasize traits or qualities such as fairness, honesty or mischievousness.*

▶ *Growing up and the people they met.*

▶ *Their career, their interests, their achievements.*

▶ *Their family.*

▶ *Their beliefs – religious, humanist or whatever.*

▶ *Their effect on people that they met. Their effect and impact on you and your life.*

▶ *Thanking them for sharing their life and impacting on all of the people present.*

▶ *How much they will be sadly missed.*

Delivering a funeral speech is understandably a daunting process, especially if you are the bereaved person. If you do not feel able to speak then do not worry; it is perfectly understandable and reasonable for you to ask someone else to do so. A clergyman or a lay reader or a humanist reader will be able to do so on your behalf and may even read out a funeral speech that you have written, if that is your wish.

Yet if you are able to deliver the speech, do not worry if your voice quavers or cracks. That is a normal emotion that all will accept and know that it is because you are feeling emotional. Here is probably a good time to think about how we talk to someone who has recently been bereaved. The thing is that there are several definite stages of grief and depending upon which stage they are in they may react differently.

The grief process

Many people do not like to talk about death and as a consequence are ill prepared for the changing emotions that they experience during bereavement. The normal grief process lasts for about three months. There will still be emotional pain, but things will become easier.

The following are the normal grief stages:

1   Initial shock – *the person cannot accept that the person has gone; they may even exhibit the mental mechanism of 'denial' whereby they refuse to believe that the person has died. This shock is often accompanied by emotional blunting, so that the person does not weep as much as they would expect, or they just cannot cry. Do not be alarmed; it will pass.*
2   Yearning – *this comes after a few days. The person yearns and wants the deceased person to come back. They find themselves filled with memories and images. They want to be close to their things and personal effects. During this time, which can last for a week or two, there is often anger that the person has been taken away, that certain people did not do enough, etc. The anger is usually not justified. Then there is guilt; perhaps the person feels that if only they had done certain things the individual would still be with them. Guilt about things that had not been said before the person died.*
3   Despair – *this can last a few more weeks. This is the sadness that comes when it is realized that they have gone. It is common for people to hibernate, to become apathetic and to feel that life is pointless. But all this will pass.*
4   Recovery – *as the main hurting starts to go. It is a matter of coming to terms with the loss so that one can start to rebuild one's life.*

Persuasive speech

Some speeches have to persuade an audience towards a particular point of view. They may be the speeches in a debate, or in a political context or as part of a health campaign, or in business.

Think of such a speech as having three parts.

1. THE INTRODUCTION

This is the hook, the attention grabber. You should aim to deliver the message that you want to deliver in a memorable manner. In a sentence or two say it in a way that gets the audience to think. That is, you hook their attention.

For example, if you want people to stop smoking don't just start out saying that smoking is bad for you. Everyone knows that already. People smoke, they live in denial and imagine that the awful illnesses that it causes will not happen to them because they feel well at the moment.

No, if you want to hook them then you might have to appeal to their concern for their family, their children and what would happen to them if they were left parentless. The audience might not be in that age group, may not have a family, yet you can still hook them if you can personalize the introduction. For example, you could tell them (as long as it is true) that '…it happened to a friend (or relative) of mine. He died from a smoking-related disease and left his wife and three children without insurance and without an income.'

2. THE MIDDLE

Here you expand on the statement that you made and you then move from the story to list the problems associated with it. Or, of course, if you are trying to persuade people to buy a product or take up some new way of doing something, then you talk about the benefits. Provide the evidence you have for each problem or benefit.

Asking rhetorical questions (questions with only one logical answer) will keep bringing them back to the original topic, while using persuader words such as 'surely', 'truly', 'clearly' and 'obviously' will strengthen your message.

3. THE CONCLUSION

Here you bring it all together, neatly showing how the evidence you have given leads them irrefutably to the conclusion that they must do whatever you are trying to persuade them to do.

After-dinner speaking

Eloquent speakers are much sought after to enliven and entertain after a social dinner. Sportsmen, politicians, actors and comedians can make sizeable amounts of money by exercising their larynx at such an event. You may not be asked to give a huge after-dinner speech – it may be just a short talk after the annual society dinner – yet with a set of strategies you can always give a creditable performance.

The first thing to remember is that this is a performance. The way that you look and sound matter more than the things you say. After you read this section go back to Chapter 7, 'How you look, act and say', and refresh your memory.

Your nerves may be a bit fraught at the prospect, yet there is no real reason to worry. People will have had a good dinner and perhaps a drink or two, so they will be on your side and will be quite receptive.

People worry about hecklers at dinners. If it is a formal dinner then this is unlikely. If it is a sports club dinner, then it is almost certainly going to be an occasion when you will get some. Yet it will not be malicious heckling, but good-natured banter. Just have a few little one-liners ready for any hecklers.

If heckled, try these:

▶ 'Ah, a heckler. I thought this was a refined dinner. Who let the riff-raff in?'

▶ 'Why, what was that? Did I hear a wit? No, it must have just been a half-wit.'

▶ 'Goodness, who bought … a ticket for a do like this? He hasn't been known to pay for anything before. In fact, the moths in his wallet have never learned how to fly.'

And if someone repeats something that another heckler has called out:

▶ 'Oh, we have an echo here. I hope it was just an echo and not someone trying to be funny….' (Point to first heckler.) '… It was only slightly funny when he said it. It's not remotely funny a second time. People are shaking their heads at you.'

You don't have to be nasty, just firm. And always smile at them, not smugly, but pleasantly.

Here are a few hints for an after-dinner speech:

▶ Pitch your speech appropriately – *Consider the reason for the dinner. Is it a celebration, an anniversary or a sort of ritual? This will determine what sort of a speech they will expect. A professional group will expect you to adopt a professional tone. That means be polite, be efficient and be just a little bit laid back. A sports club or interest club of some sort will probably be more relaxed. They are quite likely going to be more accepting of humour.*
▶ Know your audience – *If you have been asked to speak but have no prior knowledge of the group, then ask your host, or the person who invited you, a few questions. How many people will*

be there? What is the dress code? What is the mix of the sexes? Always err on the side of caution with the things that you say. Do not take risks with ill-thought-out jokes. Do not swear; it merely shows a lack of erudition and no one will think better of you for knowing swear words.

▶ Know about the venue – *Is it a closed restaurant? A hall? A single table in a restaurant with other paying diners? You need to know about these things so that you can plan your talk. If it is going to be a room that other people are dining in, then they may not want to hear your ribald jokes, or your recital of 'Tam o'Shanter'. Have consideration for them.*

▶ How long have you got? – *It is very important to know that they don't want you to go on too long. A short few words would just be three or four minutes. Most speeches take nine or ten minutes, which is probably going to be right. Fifteen minutes would be a long speech on such occasions. If it is a sporting occasion and prizes are going to be given out, then do aim to keep it short. Long speeches are only going to be expected if they have paid you a hefty fee and you are a renowned after-dinner speaker.*

▶ Prepare what you are going to say – *This is the same with a presentation, a book reading or any other type of public speaking. If you want to look good and seem professional, then do what the professionals do and practise. Again, look at Chapter 7 on 'How you look, act and say' and Chapter 13 on Presentations. Practise, practise, practise – let those three words be your mantra.*

One thing about notes – it is probably better to prepare bullet points on cards rather than come with wads of paper. People will groan if they think that they are going to hear someone drone on as they read from their notes. Be subtle with the cards. Place them on the table and use them as prompts. You will, after all, have practised.

Have a witty little introduction. An anecdote about how you came to be asked, what you were doing at the time, and how talking before such an illustrious group was the last thing that you had on your mind. Then mention your credentials or otherwise for making such a speech. This can be mildly amusing.

The purpose of the dinner will, as I said above, give you the clue as to what sort of talk it is to be. Are people there to be:

▶ *Entertained? In which case you are definitely there as a* performer.
▶ *Informed? In this case you are the expert on something and are an* informer.
▶ *Reformed? In which case you are there as a* persuader.

Most speeches will benefit from a joke. Try to make it a fitting one for the audience and keep it clean and crisp. Have a look at Chapter 11, 'It's how you tell them'.

Have a summary of your talk. If it is a society event, say how the year has been in a couple of lines. Thank everyone for the parts they played. And thank the audience for their welcome, their attention and their benevolence in listening to you.

Bow and wait for the applause.

Saying thank you

This can sometimes fill people with trepidation. But it should not. There is nothing that can go wrong. The audience have already listened to someone else speak and you are just being asked to say thank you.

It should not be a speech in itself. Thank the person for what they have done and the way that they have done it. Then say that you are sure that you speak for everyone present in saying how enjoyable it has been (or words to that effect) and that they have your thanks.

As you start to applaud, so will everyone else.

Before every type of speech, even a simple thank-you at the end of someone else's talk, you should practice, practice and practice in front of the mirror.

Prepare patter for the start of every speech.

15

Be assertive in conflict

Many people are told that they should be more assertive. If you assert yourself, then all of your problems will be over. At least that is what is implied in the sort of magazine articles that you read while sitting in waiting rooms.

It is not as easy as that, however. For one thing, the attribute of being assertive is not easy to pin down. It means different things to different people. For some it conjures up an image of being brave. Others see it as being blunt, aggressive or argumentative.

A lot of people wish that they were more assertive, while others imagine that they already are. Where do you stand on this?

Wimp, warrior or wizard?

Before we go any further, just consider a few questions. Be brutally honest with yourself:

▶ *Have you ever come away from a situation or even avoided one altogether because you did not feel that you could stand your corner in a discussion or argument?*
▶ *Do you feel that you let people walk all over you?*
▶ *Do you feel that you don't stand up for yourself, or that you don't put forward your point of view or your side of the argument?*

- ▶ *Do you worry that you will be steamrollered in an argument?*
- ▶ *Do you feel that you will be humiliated by people in an argument?*
- ▶ *Do you fester and seethe afterwards?*
- ▶ *Do you plot to get even?*
- ▶ *Do you complain afterwards to someone else?*
- ▶ *Do you show your anger to someone else and say what you're going to do next time?*
- ▶ *Do you have sleepless nights going over and over the same scene, only this time saying the things that would have put the other person in their place and made you feel better about yourself?*

If the answer to a most of those questions is yes, then I guess you have long since wished that you were just a bit more assertive. By that you mean you wish you could stand your corner and give the other person a good telling-off.

You feel that you are a wimp and you would like to be a warrior.

On the other hand:

- ▶ *Do you find yourself leaping in where angels fear to tread?*
- ▶ *Do you see red and frequently complain in shops, restaurants or bars?*
- ▶ *Do you tell people exactly what you think of them?*
- ▶ *Do you think it is good to give people a good telling-off?*
- ▶ *Do you really lose your temper?*
- ▶ *Afterwards, when your temper has calmed down, do you feel good?*
- ▶ *Afterwards do you feel full of remorse?*
- ▶ *Afterwards do you ever think you have gone too far?*
- ▶ *Have you ever alienated others or soured a relationship for ever because of your temper?*

This is another extreme. You may feel that you are a warrior. You may feel that you win by bludgeoning the other person into submission. Or you may be generally calm and quiet, shy even, yet when pushed you let people know that you are a warrior. Of course, if you feel bad afterwards then there has to be a reason. That reason may be that you feel bad about losing your temper. It could also be because you actually made an almighty hash of a situation through simple blind rage and rant. Your outburst did not settle the matter.

My point is that often people who associate with one of those extreme types of behaviour may wish they were more like the other. Life would be simpler for the wimp if he could be a warrior. Rather like the old adverts one used to see of seven-stone weaklings getting sand kicked in their face on the beach, then months later, after some get-fit-quick regime, they do the same to the bully-boy. On the other hand, the warrior may wish that if he could just bite his tongue, be more wimpish then he could save himself a lot of angst.

Yet both of them should really wish that they could be more like some friend who never flaps, never loses it, but who keeps calm, says just the right thing and seems to enjoy a life of equanimity. That person may be no more intelligent, yet somehow, almost magically, they can sort things out without seeming to lose their temper. Don't you think that it would be better to be a wizard, for that is how I see this type, rather than a wimp or a warrior?

Of course you do. Well, you can be like that person if you just understand and apply a little strategy. It is a good idea to assess where you are, but not with any psychometric test. I don't believe that you need to quantify things like this, just get a good feel for your own natural tendencies. You can do it yourself.

In Chapter 12 on 'Winning arguments' we looked at Sheldon's somatotypes. It is a rule of thumb only. So too is this rough categorization of wimps, warriors and wizards. You may not like the three words, because they may seem to be an over-simplification, yet if you are the type of person who has trouble talking you may have a number of misconceptions about them.

WIMPS

The first type of person that we looked at is often categorized as a wimp. It is a pejorative term, rather like 'coward' or 'chicken'. It is a concept, if not a term, that many people's inner critic uses for them and which it brandishes at the front of their mind whenever a potential confrontational situation starts to loom large:

'You're not up to it.'
'You'll look a fool.'
'He or she will make mincemeat of you.'

Well, from your reading of Chapter 3, 'Silence your inner critic', you know what you need to do, don't you? You need to challenge him. Show him that things are not as he imagines. You are not that person who is going to be browbeaten. You are not a fool. And you are not a wimp!

In fact, what a silly word it is. The *Oxford English Dictionary* defines it as 'a feeble or ineffectual person'. Its origin is vague, but is believed to come from the behaviour of such a person and their tendency to whimper.

In fact, I don't think that people should think of themselves as wimps. While I have suggested above that you should see where you are, I really mean that it is a useful starting point, I do not think it is how you should actually categorize yourself. That is just playing into the hands of the inner critic. No, accept that you may exhibit and use wimpish behaviour in areas of your life, but forget the idea that you are a wimp.

So what is wimpish behaviour? It can mean a lot of things:

▶ *Avoiding arguments at all costs*
▶ *Avoiding all confrontations*
▶ *Never taking a risk*

- *Agreeing even when you think differently*
- *Showing nervousness*
- *Never putting yourself forward*
- *Never volunteering*
- *Complaining behind someone's back*
- *Whining*
- *Whinging.*

There is nothing wrong with avoiding arguments or confrontations a lot of the time, but sometimes it is important to stand up for what you think is right. Similarly, you do not have to volunteer for things. You may not have time, or you may have no interest in a particular activity.

Complaining behind people's backs, whining and whinging are different, however. They are unpleasant characteristics. People express their anger that way, often doing so in a light that will make them look justified in their outrage. But why are they expressing their anger to a third party like this? Perhaps it is because the object of their ire is more powerful, older or higher up the pecking order.

If you have ever felt this and you recognize that you do adopt this kind of behaviour, then you should try to see that it is inappropriate behaviour. It is poor communication. In fact, it is non-communication. There is nothing wrong with putting your point forward in an appropriate manner. You don't need to be a warrior, you can be a wizard.

WARRIORS

Now this word sounds altogether more desirable. It conjures up images of brave folk doing brave things. Hercules, Sir Lancelot, Sir Winston Churchill, and all of the good people who stand up for the downtrodden and who get out there and achieve results.

Note that word 'achieve' because it is important. Being a warrior isn't just someone who goes into combat, be that physical or verbal, it is someone who does so in a skilled manner.

If you are a skilled warrior who achieves a good result then that is great. I cannot do anything for you. You simply don't need any help. On the other hand, a lot of people who think that they are warriors are not really. They are simply bullish, bullying, hot-heads, and more than likely just wimps in disguise.

This wimpish aggression, as I like to call it, is also an inefficient method of communication and is liable to get you a reputation. People may feel that they never know when you might blow up. The fact is that you do not need to blow up or erupt with rage. That is almost always counter-productive. Learn to be a wizard.

WIZARDS

When I talk about being a wizard I do not mean that you have to be magical. What you need to be able to do is to transform a bad or ugly confrontation into an effective communication. It is being diplomatic and statesmanlike in such situations.

Assertiveness is about being polite

You should emblazon this on your memory. Assertiveness has nothing to do with rudeness. You should aim to be polite, but positive.

A balanced person who stands his or her ground and speaks politely, but firmly is someone who understands being assertive. Shouting, screaming, hissing, being blunt and giving people a tongue-lashing are not ways of being assertive; they are reactions and behaviour patterns that do not truly assert a positive position. By staying calm and presenting a firm manner and talking politely you will convey a powerful message.

Avoid gunfighting

Let's start with aggression. This really is important because so many people misconstrue aggression for assertion. In their attempt to be assertive they may simply come across as being aggressive. If we go back to the ideas discussed in Chapter 7 on 'How you look, act and say', you will see how this can be very relevant in any confrontational situation. Your demeanour will tell people how you are feeling and how you are about to act.

In old-fashioned western gunfights, the films always showed that the bad guy – who draws first – always loses to the good guy, who outmanoeuvres him. This fascinated the Nobel Prize–winning physicist Niels Bohr who showed that it seemed to be true. The intentional act of drawing and shooting takes longer to perform than the action in response. Interestingly, research at Birmingham University recently backs this up.

In developing his theory about the gunfighter's dilemma Niels Bohr postulated that since both gunfighters knew that the first to draw is unlikely to win, neither would want to draw first, and so the logical thing to do would be to talk.

This is a good thing to keep in mind. Shooting from the hip is a bad strategy. You go off without adequate thinking and take a shot at the other person. Very often the shot does more harm than good. It is a wild shot. Also very often there will be an immediate response, and, as with the gunfighter analogy, there is a good chance that the response will be fast too, or you will not have sufficient ammunition to return fire after that. You will not have considered the whole thing properly.

Avoid put-downs

Surely, the put-down is just what you really want. This is a misconception. Dishing out a good put-down is not being assertive; it is just being vindictive. You do not want to use put-downs because they are unpleasant to receive and they will mark you as a bully.

To put down someone is to demonstrate that you are in a superior position to someone. They are often things delivered by people who have an edge, some authority over someone else. They will do nothing but create bad feeling. The other person will remember it and like you less for it. No one ever admires a put-down merchant.

Avoid sarcasm
I have mentioned this before in Chapter 11. It is said to be the lowest form of wit. No one except the sarcastic person ever sees humour in sarcasm. It is always directed at someone to belittle them, to make them feel small and inferior.

Don't be tactless
People often don't think about the effects their words may have on someone else. Most people are more sensitive than they like others to imagine. It is a defence that we all tend to develop to some degree or another. The truth is that even the most seemingly rhinoceros-skinned individual is capable of being hurt to the quick!

Do not be flippant or derogatory about other people's abilities, their looks, their likes, beliefs, race or sex. Don't preface things with phrases like 'Let me be blunt' or 'Let me be brutally honest'.

Why would you say that unless your intention is to be deliberately hurtful or cruel? And why would you expect someone to stand there and accept that? It is a bit like saying, 'Let me just hit you in the face.'

Avoid accusations
Making accusations means that the other person will immediately have to defend their position. Sometimes of course it is the correct thing to do, such as when you have seen someone commit a crime

or engage in a deliberate act to harm or hurt someone. In general, however, adopting an accusatory tone is an act of aggression.

Finger jabbing, pointing, hand waving and thumping fists into the palm are all aggressive body movements and are best avoided. Why are you feeling the need to show anger? If you are having to do that then you are in danger of losing your temper and with it the discussion.

People march into shops, toss things that they purchase down on the counter and demand a refund. They castigate shop assistants for making mistakes. Why show anger in such circumstances? It will not show you in a good light.

There are always better and more pleasant ways to do things.

Don't give people the silent treatment
Call it the brush-off, the cold shoulder, or the silent treatment, this is a curious behaviour that serves no useful purpose at all, other than to show you to be surly and unwilling to engage in fruitful and constructive communication.

The PEA strategy

This is another acronym and another little strategy to use when faced with a confrontational situation. Each letter of the word PEA stands for three things:

▶ *Problem, Position and Politeness*
▶ *Expectation, Equality and Equanimity*
▶ *Answer, Aim, Achieve.*

It is as simple as that, yet it is one of the best approaches you can adopt when you feel that you need to discuss a point with someone.

Just giving someone a telling-off, a piece of your mind, or giving them an earful of your ire will not resolve a conflict or confrontation. It will achieve very little. Note that word – *achieve*. The thing is that if you are going to engage in a conflict or confrontation then you do need to have some sort of idea what it is all about. Just unleashing a purple haze will resolve nothing and will do little to achieve anything except discord and unpleasantness.

The PEA strategy is the way of the diplomat. Let's go through the strategy.

THE THREE PS

First, define the *problem*. What exactly is the difficulty? You will need to be quite specific and not just formulate it in general terms. If you have an issue with someone at work, for example, then what is the problem? Is it a question of their behaviour? You need to have a specific example, not just an accusatory statement about them in general. If there is an issue about bullying behaviour, then you need a specific example.

The position relates to how the problem affects your *position* in the state of affairs. If it is a work issue with someone, then how does it affect your ability to work with them or to fulfil your role?

Try to be dispassionate about this and not bring emotion into it. Emotion is exactly what you are trying to keep out of the discussion. It can be brought in afterwards, but in the first instance, it needs to be a simple factual statement about how it affects your position.

Politeness is utterly essential. If you are polite and do not lose your temper or demonstrate inappropriate emotions then you will be able to stand your ground credibly. You will demonstrate assertiveness.

THE THREE ES

First, *expectation*. That means your expectation of the other person. What exactly do you expect of them? What do you expect them to change in order to resolve the situation? Once again, you need to be specific about what change will demonstrate that to you. Don't be general and say 'a change of attitude' or 'being more efficient'.

What aspect of attitude do you mean? What one thing could they do that would make them more efficient?

You need to know what you expect and be able to formulate it in such as way that they will be able to comprehend how the situation can be resolved. Talking about a general attitude is a direct attack that leaves little room for manoeuvre on the part of the other person, and you should always leave them room to do so.

Equality means adopting an equal position in this discussion. Saying 'Let's discuss this', rather than 'I have a bone to pick with you', is far more likely to get things onto an even footing and an equal and measured discussion than if you go in with an accusatory or inflammatory tone.

Equanimity means striving to remain calm, composed and level-headed throughout. Even if the other person is heated, then your equanimity, your balance will throw them off their stride. If someone is calm, like that wizard friend of yours, and does not flap or lose their cool, then an angry person will start to feel uncertain of their anger and possibly slightly foolish.

THE THREE AS

First, *answer*. You must let them answer; otherwise you are just having a rant, which is going to go nowhere. You need to give them that opportunity so that you can then explain, calmly, why their attitude, or whatever it is that you have an issue with, is causing you to have a problem.

Your *aim* is to achieve a satisfactory answer to the issue that is causing the problem. That aim should have mutual benefits for you both, since this should not be regarded as a battle. You should aim to allow the other person to have some say in the way that you will resolve the issue – together.

Finally, *achieve*. You will achieve your goal if you come away maintaining that sense of equanimity that you have gone to pains to convey. You will have achieved a successful outcome if you have allowed them to feel part of the process. And you will have achieved a magical answer to the problem because you will both have reached the solution.

WHAT IF YOU ARE THE PERSON THAT SOMEONE HAS AN ISSUE WITH?

This may well happen, of course, since none of us is perfect and you may ruffle someone's feathers.

Well, you still use PEA. Suppose someone suddenly stomps into your office, your group at the bar or club, or into your shop and starts verbally tearing into you? What do you do? Like a gunfighter do you fire back straight away? Preferably not. Your first move is to calm the situation.

Smile – a welcoming smile, not one that could be perceived as smug or condescending. Then try to be conciliatory. That is not the same as being cowardly or wimpish. Your aim is to defuse the situation and show that you are willing to discuss the situation.

Simple phases like 'let's discus this' or 'well, all problems can be solved' will tend to take the steam out of the process.

Follow the PEA strategy:

The three Ps

▶ *Ask what the* problem *is, then, if it is hurled back at you that your attitude is the issue, ask for a little specificity.*
▶ *Think also about how this is affecting your* position *and how it is affecting the other person's position.*
▶ *Be* polite *throughout.*

The three Es

▶ *Ask what their* expectation *is. What are they hoping from you, and think how it will relate to your expectation.*
▶ *Be prepared to discuss this as* equals.
▶ *Maintain* equanimity *throughout.*

The three As

▶ Answer *without losing your temper. Try to formulate your answer so that it actually is an answer to their question, rather than just a defensive manoeuvre.*
▶ Aim *to achieve peace and understanding.*
▶ Achieve *a defusing of the situation, a formulation of what the issues were and a plan as to how you can both achieve a reasonable outcome.*

Strategy

Remember that a good wizard uses PEA in any conflict or confrontation.

16

Interviews

In these difficult days when jobs are scarce most people feel exhilarated to be called for an interview. Then they start to worry about the ordeal ahead. The very thought of sitting in front of a panel of people and being grilled fills many with dread. It need not, because this is another of those situations when preparation will give you the best chance of showing off your personality and skills to the best advantage. Once again, it's about performance.

A successful interview requires you to perform to the very best of your ability. You have to demonstrate why you, rather than all of the other candidates, are the right person for the job or position.

Gone are the days of patronage and nepotism when you could just be given a job. Equal opportunities means that positions have to be advertised. A job application is a competition and, depending on how many posts are available, there will be one or more winners and probably very many more who are not successful.

Note that way of putting it – 'not successful' rather than 'losers'. That is the correct way of looking at this since an unsuccessful result does not make one a loser. The people who gain the position have won the post, but they are not necessarily any better qualified for the post than the other applicants; they have just come across better at the interview stage. That is the way that it is these days, you see. By the time of the interview most employers will have gone through a large process of selection and rejection of CVs. Your first part in the process should have been to prepare the very best and most honest CV that you can.

Your curriculum vitae

Your curriculum vitae is one of the most important documents that you make in your life. It is a Latin term, meaning 'course of life'. It is essentially a résumé of one's educational attainments, work record and interests, and is something that is generally required when applying for posts.

It has to be a true reflection of all of these things:

▶ *Never claim what you have not achieved.*
▶ *Never claim interests that you do not have.*
▶ *Never profess expertise that you do not have.*
▶ *Never claim experience that you do not have.*
On the other hand:
▶ *Always put in what you have achieved.*
▶ *Always ensure that you have documentary evidence of your achievements.*
▶ *Always make sure that it is word perfect with no spelling mistakes.*
▶ *Always make sure that it is up to date.*
▶ *Always make sure that the copy you give is a fresh one.*

The CV is not just a few sheets of stapled paper or a small file of stuff about you that you never look at. Nor is it something that you don't care about. The CV is *you*!

Or rather, it is as much of you that the selection panel see, unless you are applying for a position internally in an organization or company where you are already well known. Yet, even then, it is the opportunity that you have been given to explain a lot about yourself. You should therefore make it as interesting as possible. That means as interesting as possible to prospective employers. As much as you can, you are going to have to try to get inside their heads as you prepare the CV.

Make sure that you include all of your qualifications. Make doubly sure that you have outlined all of your interests, as long as none are in any way anti-social.

Do not make the mistake of thinking that is all there is to the CV. It is not just a key to get you the interview. The CV is going to be a main part of the interview, so you should know it back to front and inside out. You have to be able to talk about every single item without a moment's hesitation. And you must be able to do so with enthusiasm.

PREPARING TO ANSWER QUESTIONS ON YOUR CV

A friend or relative can help you with this. Get them to ask you questions about your CV. It is not difficult for them simply to go through it almost entry by entry, and just say, 'So tell me a little about your education' or 'What made you select those subjects for A level?' Or, 'Tell me a little about your interest in canoeing.'

You should prepare little pieces of patter for each one. Then go to your large mirror, sit down as you would in an interview and ask yourself each of those questions and watch yourself give your patter.

Rehearsal is fundamental and I will come back to that soon.

....

Top Tip
Your CV is you, so you must be able to answer questions on it instantly.
....

Self-esteem

You are going to be selling yourself at the interview. If you are going to successfully sell anything you have to believe in your product. When you sell yourself you have to believe that you are the best person for the position.

You have to like yourself, otherwise poor self-esteem will show. So start getting ready and enjoy being you. Look at all of the things that you have done, the things that make you the person that you are. Whether or not you actually feel that you have achieved your potential or not, start liking yourself.

By that I mean that you should look at all of the positives in your life, not the negatives. You may have wanted to become a professional sports person, yet never achieved that dream. You may have wanted to write a best-selling novel, but as yet have never had a single article published. Those things don't matter, really they don't. They are things you aspire to and whether or not they have been achieved does not affect your own self-worth. You are a valuable person. You are a member of society. You contribute in many ways.

Believe in yourself; take pride in your abilities, in your appearance and in the dreams. Use your mirror and see your good points. They are the building bricks to construct the persona that you want the interview panel to see and like.

Preparing for the interview

Apart from knowing your CV back to front, there is plenty of other preparation that you can – indeed, should – do for the big day.

RESEARCH

Believe it or not, there are people who fire off a raft of CVs to different prospective employers and get interviews, only to show remarkable ignorance about the job that they have applied for and of their abilities to do the job. Even worse, they unforgivably know nothing about the organization that they have approached in the hope of gaining a job or position.

There is no excuse in this day and age for not checking up on the organization. You can find out lots of information about the type of organization it is, or about the organization itself from a little Internet research. Look up the company's website. Find out, if you can, who the personnel are, what their different functions are and also what the job you are applying for entails. If you are not adept on the computer then get someone else to help you. If you do not do this, then you risk appearing ill-prepared and uninterested.

Remember, you have to sell yourself and that means that you have to show that you are enthusiastic, that you have initiative and that you have the capabilities of using technology.

There is absolutely nothing wrong in contacting the organization yourself and asking whether you can come and have a look around. If you do that, go prepared with some questions, but not with *all* of your questions. Hold some back for the interview itself.

If you can get there ahead of the interview it is a definite help if you get the opportunity to speak to someone in the department that you are applying to join. They may be able to give some information about the job that could be helpful to you. Knowing how the job vacancy arose, for example, how secure it will be, and so on.

PREPARE SOME ANSWERS FOR THE INTERVIEW

The interviewers will almost certainly be looking for certain attributes in a person that will equip them to do the job. They may very well have a tick-box list.

The first few moments of the interview will probably involve the panellists introducing themselves or being introduced by the main interviewer. It is usual for one or two pleasantries to be exchanged. You must be polite and prepared to answer confidently, but succinctly. Don't try to impress them by going off on an irrelevant little diatribe about the weather or the state of the transport system. You have arrived, had a look around and they do not want your first few words to be moans.

The ball is then going to be firmly in your court, because this is where they will ask you about your CV. You will already have patter prepared and will be able to expand as much as they want to hear. Be careful about being too enthusiastic about your social life and how much you like partying, however. Remember that you are there seeking employment, and they are likely to want to employ someone who is going to be reliable, not someone who may come in with frequent hangovers.

With some careful thought you should be able to anticipate some of the questions that they are going to ask.

'Why do you want to work for us?'
This should slip off the tongue as a piece of well-prepared patter. Your research into the way that the company makes soap interests you because 'everyone is interested in hygiene'. You have a particular interest in the science behind the product (which you should also research) and even though you chose to do arts subjects at college and were attracted into marketing, it still intrigues you, and as someone interested in marketing you are sure that it is a product that will sell. 'And another thing of course is your company statement about ecology and ethically produced goods...' etc., etc.

'What qualities do you think that you would bring to this job?'
Again this is not the sort of thing that you want to be umming and ahing about at that moment. It should have been thought out and tailored to the company or organization you want to join.

Your research into the organization has told you that the organization is committed to providing humanitarian aid to developing countries – 'This is a subject close to my heart. I support several charities (be truthful) and have always wanted to work in the charity sector...I believe that your mission statement reflects my own philosophy and outlook on life...If selected I am sure that I will bring the right attitude to the job...I have enthusiasm and passion for the work that you are doing ...I believe that good enthusiastic clerical work is essential in any charity organization and I am sure that I would fit in...I am a people person and this is a people-oriented organization...' etc., etc.

'What has been your greatest achievement in your career so far?'
This is a standard question at most interviews. It is no time for modesty. Have it ready up your sleeve and deliver it crisply. Think of something you have done of which you are proud. Be able to talk about it and explain why it was such an achievement.

'What has been your biggest failure?'
This is another common question. It is designed to show that you can acknowledge errors and also show that you can describe a difficult episode swiftly and capably.

The question is also designed to show what you learned from that failure. If they don't ask that, then make sure that you volunteer an answer. Show that you learn from mistakes and that you always use experiences as opportunities to learn. If you can tell them how it improved what you do in some way then that is going to get you brownie points.

'What is your dream job?'
Do not immediately say 'This one!' That is the expected response, but not the one that they want. They want you to be a bit more imaginative. This may be the dream job, but what you should do is describe the things that are important to you, in the area that you have applied and, if the job in question is close, then you say it.

Do not say that the position is not exactly your dream job but that it will do until something else comes along. You can indicate that it seems to be the sort of job that would give you experience in order to progress towards your dream job.

The other thing you must not say is that your dream job is something totally different.

THE INTERVIEW – A TWO-WAY PROCESS

It is generally a good thing to interact with your interviewers, so long as you do not end up overplaying your hand and end up seeming to interview them.

At suitable points if you have a question about something that needs clarification, then ask. Also have a few questions ready for them. Obvious things will relate to holidays, salary and flexibility of the job. It is generally not a good idea to start with these. Better to ask more enthusiastic questions first. You might consider asking them what their policy is on health and safety, first aid, pensions, smoking. How would they describe the management structure of the organization? What is there view on team-building? Are there any in-house training opportunities? If you are successful who would your boss be and what is the line of management? Again, don't overdo it. Three or four questions at the most will be enough.

Finally, don't forget that you may be the right person for them, but are they right for you? You don't have to accept the position if it is offered. You may need time to think about it.

Top Tip
When you are asked if you have any questions, ask only 3 or 4 sensible ones. Any more than that is unlikely to be welcome.

REMEMBER IT IS HOW YOU LOOK THAT WILL BE NOTICED

You need to look smart. It doesn't matter what the job is, you need to look presentable and smart. It may be a graphic design firm or a computer game company where everyone dresses casually, but if you attend for interview, you must look professional and smart. That means clean and well groomed. Casual perhaps if everyone is casual, but it has to be smart casual. No dirty trainers, no jeans, no beanie hats or baseball caps.

...AND HOW YOU ACT

You are going to act the part of the person who wants the job, the person who is right for the job, and the person who is pleased to be there and who looks as if they are going to fit in well.

Do read Chapter 7 on 'How you look, act and say' again before an interview. It is so important that you convey the right image. This means rehearsal in front of the mirror. You have to rehearse how you come into the room, how you greet each person, with a good firm, but not too firm, handshake, with good eye contact and with a relaxed demeanour.

Do take some extra copies of your CV, just in case someone on the panel does not have one. Show that you are proud of it.

Rehearse sitting down on an upright chair, with your legs uncrossed and with your hands resting lightly on your knees. Show respect, but quiet confidence.

Eye contact is of paramount importance as usual. Make sure that you have good contact with whoever is asking you a question, then between times make sure that you make eye contact with the other panellists. Don't stare at them, but do look at them, and be prepared to smile. Not a gushing smile but a friendly one.

Do not:

- ▶ *sit looking too casual*
- ▶ *sit with legs crossed so that an ankle is resting on a knee*
- ▶ *lean forward and rest your forearms on the table*
- ▶ *sit back with your hands behind your head and your legs stretched out*
- ▶ *do anything anti-social – no chewing gum, scratching, picking your nose.*

...AND HOW YOU SAY THINGS

While in many situations your actual words are not the main thing that people focus on, in an interview they are going to be listening very closely to the account you give of yourself.

Be prepared for the scenario questions
It is highly likely that you will be asked what you would do in a variety of situations. They will all appertain to the job you are going for, so there is no need to worry. You should be able to anticipate them.

If you are going for a job as a teaching assistant you will be asked about situations to do with children or their parents. Some will be very obvious, but some may be designed to stretch you. For example, you may be asked what you would say or how you would react if a child demonstrated inappropriate behaviour to another child. Or what would your reaction be if a parent expressed racist views. Such questions will not be designed to trip you up; they are aimed at eliciting what your own views are and also that you are au fait with what is and is not acceptable behaviour in society today.

Be careful about revealing quirks
This might sound a bit odd, but it is important that you do not say anything that could make people think that you hold rigid views, a particular political persuasion, or that you are intolerant

of any group. You should aim to come across as a thinking, open-minded person.

The result

'WE WOULD LIKE TO OFFER YOU THE POSITION'

That may be music to your ears. Perhaps you have been waiting ages to get this job, or any job.

Before you snap their hands off, do consider whether it is actually a good deal. There is a problem about taking a job and then moving on soon after. You get a reputation as a rolling ball and it will show on your CV. Do you need time to consider? Talk with a partner, perhaps?

If, at the end of the day, it is what you were looking for, then congratulations.

'WE ARE SORRY, YOUR APPLICATION WAS UNSUCCESSFUL'

Don't go away and drown your sorrows, or go home and kick the proverbial cat. You may have just been pipped at the post. Or, you may have been totally wrong for them, or you may have come across badly for some reason.

Ask for feedback, since it is always useful. You can build on that. Do not take it personally. In the current job market it is difficult to get new jobs and you must not take it as a personal slight. Someone else got the job on the day that is all.

Keep your chin up, look after your self-esteem and eventually you will be successful.

17

Talking to authority

Strong reasons make strong actions.

William Shakespeare, *King John*

Many people hate the idea of talking to authority figures. Bosses, managers, police officers, lawyers, judges, teachers, dentists, bank managers – they are considered authority figures by many folk. Why should you be anxious about talking to them?

Well, if you have committed some crime you probably have every right to feel anxious about talking to the police. If the situation escalates then you may need to speak to a lawyer and, worse, you may find yourself in court, in front of a magistrate or even a judge.

If you are in the right, then you should have nothing to fear, of course. On the other hand, if you are in the wrong and you know it, then you may have some ill-tasting medicine to swallow.

In general though, there is no real reason why you should fear speaking to anyone. People associate uniforms with authority, and it is usually the uniform or the mantle that goes with a job that people react to. In other words the position carries with it some social position, expectation or power. Indeed, it is the last word that is generally the most important because it is when people feel that they are in a position of subservience to someone with more power than themselves that they feel cowed and tongue-tied.

Jungian archetypes

I touched on Carl Jung, the founder of analytical psychology, in Chapter 3. It is worth considering his theories a little further since it can be helpful in understanding why we tend to view some people, or rather some people's occupations or positions in society with awe. Jung would have said that we are programmed that way.

Jung taught that the ego was the conscious awareness part of our personality. He felt that the unconscious had two components, the personal unconscious and the collective unconscious.

The personal unconscious is where our memories and feelings that we have suppressed are kept. The collective unconscious on the other hand is an inherited information bank of symbolism, concepts, drives and fears that all humans have inherited and share. Although it cannot be directly tapped into, it exerts an effect on us individually and accounts for the myths, fairy tales and the dreams that exert such a powerful hold over our imaginations. It is also the home of the archetypes that we carry around and associate with various types of figure.

Jung describes five main archetypes together with a whole raft of others that help us to fashion our own sense of the universe and the people that we meet and relate to.

The self – *this is the archetype that represents unification of conscious and unconscious.*
The shadow – *the life and sex instincts within us. The darker side of the persona that we see in stories and myths as the wild man, the weird figure that is sometimes friendly and sometimes sinister. Hard to see for he lives in shadows.*
The anima – *the female energy within the male. And the animus – the male energy within the female. Thus, according to Jung, we are never entirely male or female.*
The persona – *the image that we present to the world.*

And in addition to them there are other archetypes that we see in figures about us. Our own personal unconscious may modify how they are expressed:

- ▶ The father – *the strong, forbidding, authoritarian figure.*
- ▶ The mother – *the nurturing, comforting figure.*
- ▶ The child – *innocence, wanting to be nurtured, wanting to learn.*
- ▶ The wise old man – *the fount of knowledge, yet frail.*
- ▶ The hero – *the defender, the warrior, the knight.*
- ▶ The maiden – *innocent, desirable, distressed.*
- ▶ The trickster – *the deceiver, the liar, the mischief-maker.*

One can recognize in these the gods and characters of Roman, Greek and Teutonic mythology. One can also see how they can form images in ourselves of the powerful characters we meet in life.

Jung felt that our fears often arise from our archetypal images because we associate them with powerful individuals. What happens in our early life can bring certain archetypes to the fore, so that we learn to respect and fear certain ones. When we find ourselves confronted by an associated image of an archetype we feel disempowered and vulnerable. Talking in front of them opens us up to that vulnerability.

BUT THEY ARE ONLY PEOPLE

That is the essence of it. Someone may have a certain position, a certain occupation, but that does not mean that they have real authority over you. It is more the case that our minds create a mantle of authority that goes with the role, so that whoever is in that position is perceived to have power and authority over us. And because the archetype may be powerful in our mind, so it induces difficulty in talking to them.

Some mantles are more obvious than others, of course. A uniform is there for all to see. That is its purpose; it is showing that this individual belongs to a particular organization and that they hold a certain position within it.

Some persons have a less visible mantle, yet it is there nonetheless. Doctors, priests and lawyers don't always wear uniforms yet they sometimes induce an element of anxiety in people. And of course teachers may have it more than most, for children may grow up in awe and in some cases in fear of them.

I have said nothing of one's relationships with one's parents, but that is the most obvious mantle of all. We look to our parents for guidance, protection and nurturing as we grow up. How well they do that or not is hard to say. The way they talk to you, the way they chastise you, tell you off, or tell you to hold your tongue can all have a huge impact on the archetypes in your unconscious.

The point is that people are just people. You do not need to spend your life being fearful of the archetypes.

REMOVING THE MANTLE AND GIVING THEM SOMETHING ELSE TO WEAR

If you have a fear or difficulty of speaking to a particular type of authority figure then do not worry; you do not actually have to submit yourself to Jungian analysis to free yourself of it. You can just use the power of your own mind. It will work, but it takes time.

If you have a problem with an authority figure, say a lecturer or teacher, there is a good chance that it relates to a bad experience in the past with another teacher or someone who was involved in some aspect of your education. Think about it and try to identify that person.

Try and think about what sort of authority archetype they relate to. Is it a wise old man – a nasty old wise man, perhaps? Or could it have been someone who was deceitful, whom you couldn't trust?

That might be the trickster, you see. Or could it have been some sort of bully person that you linked with power and strength, like the hero. Only in your mind's eye now he is anything but a heroic figure. Yet you still fear him.

This is what you do. You reduce their hold over you by a little creative imagination. You go somewhere you will not be disturbed, and lie down or sit in a comfortable chair. Let yourself relax, and try to picture a stage. It is a great-looking stage such as you would see at the theatre for a pantomime.

Watch yourself come on stage to applause as the hero. It doesn't matter if you are female, because the hero or principal boy is traditionally played by a girl in pantomimes. This is our anima/animus. (Remember, it doesn't matter whether or not you accept Jung's concepts or not, it will still work if you work at it.)

You can just cavort on stage as much as you want, acting as heroically as you wish. You can, indeed, use a traditional pantomime or just invent your own. The chances are that it will have elements of all sorts of pantomimes because, of course, pantomimes are snippets from the collective unconscious.

Then, when you have your imagination working well for you, you introduce your authority figure, the one that you had the bad time with back in the past. His or her part, of course, is as the villain – the pantomime villain. The audience immediately react because they do not like him. They hiss and they boo at him. Imagine the audience full of children and parents reacting to him or her.

And he looks pathetic, miserable. The hero can literally run rings round him.

And then his doppelganger, his twin comes on stage. It is the archetype that is linked to him. Again the audience boo and hiss.

This makes the two dastardly twins cower. They feel scared and show their fear and they plead with the hero to help them out.

You agree to help them, as long as they agree to take off their robes – their 'mantles' – and dress up instead as clowns. And with a snap of your finger an old trunk zooms onto the stage. You open the lid and point to the hilarious, ridiculous clothes.

The two villains do as they are told, changing into outlandish clowns' clothing. They put on red noses. White face paint and bald pates.

The audience goes into hysterics as you magnanimously help them to hide in the trunk.

Then you push the trunk off stage with your foot and the audience cheer.

You enjoy the limelight, having de-mantled the cause of your fear and the archetype that was his twin.

Knowing that you are free of their influence, you take a bow and the curtain falls.

You may even find yourself drifting off to sleep – a very restful, satisfying sleep.

Strategy

Do this every day for a week, each time varying the pantomime, being as creative as you wish, but each time de-mantling and getting a good audience laugh. Then do it once a week, until the idea of talking with that authority figure disappears.

It is always a good thing to introduce a little test to evaluate how you have done. It shouldn't be done too soon, however. You should wait until you feel pretty sure that you cannot imagine feeling threatened by that particular authority figure again.

If your anxiety is with police officers, then the next time you are out engage a police officer in conversation. Ask for directions, for example. Just have a little small talk, just a couple of exchanges, then finish.

Dealing with bullies

This is really important because it is a sad fact that bullying behaviour is common in school, the workplace and within families. For an anxious person who has difficulty talking, if a bully gets into a position of authority, then life can become very difficult indeed.

Before we look at ways of dealing with bullies we need to consider what constitutes bullying behaviour and what makes someone a bully.

BULLYING BEHAVIOUR

You could say that bullying is just picking on someone who is unable to stand up for himself. It is actually a lot more complex that that.

Bullying is:

- *a form of abuse*
- *persistent unwanted, unwarranted criticism*
- *fault-finding*
- *nit-picking*
- *revelling in belittling someone*
- *revelling in wielding power*
- *shouting at someone*
- *being physically abusive*
- *being persistently verbally abusive*
- *taking pleasure in humiliating people*

▶ *possibly bending the truth at someone else's expense*
▶ *usually focused on an individual or a group of individuals in a vulnerable position.*

BULLIES ARE BULLIES BECAUSE THEY HAVE PROBLEMS

If you have been the brunt of bullying behaviour then you probably do not have much sympathy for the person or persons who bullied you. The fact is, however, that when someone bullies they are expressing information about their perception of themselves.

Understand first of all that a bully feels inadequate as a person. For some reason, and it will depend on what has happened in their life, they feel less than adequate. Rather than accepting that they have a problem, however, various mental mechanisms come into place to help them deal with their inadequacy.

Bullies will:

▶ *not admit that they feel inadequate*
▶ *find it difficult to accept responsibility for their behaviour*
▶ *pick on someone to show that they are superior and in their own mind are more adequate than they feel*
▶ *focus on one or more people and systematically undermine them*
▶ *chip away until they are victorious – when the other person submits or shows signs of submission.*

One of the things that you should appreciate if you are targeted by a bully is that they actually feel envious of you. It may be that you are more efficient than them, more popular or just nicer. They almost invariably have low self-esteem and are full of bitterness, jealousy and anger.

Know also that they will tend to be a serial bully, in that they will have bullied before and if you permit it they will go on to bully someone else.

DEAL WITH A BULLY WITH THE THREE CS

There are three things that you need to do when faced with bullying behaviour. They all begin with a C.

Calmness

This is important. You need to stay calm in all your dealings with them, for they are looking for the first sign that they have managed to get under your skin. Do not permit them to know that they have upset you.

In all confrontations or encounters stay calm. If they lose their temper, then they are showing that you have got under their skin. Their noise is symptomatic of their inadequacy, and they are reverting to childlike behaviour.

Faced with such a tirade, or any show of irritation, then you should mention it.

Challenge

Any outward showing of temper is inappropriate and they should be calmly challenged about it.

'You seem upset? Are you unwell?'
They may not like that, but you are challenging them about not behaving like a normal, well-adjusted person.

'You seem angry. That is not good for you.'
This also might not go down well, but it is showing them that you know that a temper tantrum or the demonstration of anger like this is a chosen behaviour – as is their bullying.

Whenever you have something levied at you, such as your competence, or your inability to perform a task, or your having failed to do something that they had asked you to do, then you should challenge them to be precise about it. Always staying calm, just ask them to show in what way the task has not been performed.

Communication
This bullying behaviour needs to be stopped in its tracks. There is always someone who can be involved or reported to. The bully may be the boss, but even he or she is generally answerable to someone else.

Communicating with others in the same position gives you safety in numbers, provided that you do something about it. That means together you should communicate the inappropriate behaviour onwards.

Being quiet and trying to put up with it without talking back will only make matters worse. The thing is that most bullies are actually quite craven when they are challenged. They may be manipulative and they may be devious and they may downright lie. You must not stoop to such behaviour. Gather whatever specific information you can, so that you can demonstrate the bullying behaviour and also ensure that you have done all the things that have been asked of you, so that you will be arguing from a position of strength if matters have to be taken further.

Top Tip
A bully is someone who has feelings of inadequacy.

When people raise their voices

As we discussed in Chapter 7 the voice is used in many ways for communication. People can vary their voice in several ways:

- ▶ *volume*
- ▶ *tempo or speed*
- ▶ *tone*
- ▶ *pitch*.

Just think how those can all be varied to express anger, joy, bewilderment and a host of other emotions. That is all about the 'how you sound' of talking. When someone is exhibiting irritation or anger they usually raise the volume, speed up the voice and alter tone and pitch.

When you want to empathize with someone, then tone-matching is the thing to do. When you want to calm someone down then you can do the reverse or modify it a little. For example, if someone is raising their voice, don't raise yours. You will need to raise it a little, but not as much as theirs. The thing is that if you just raise yours to their level then you are reacting and that is liable to maintain their fire. If you raise it to a level slightly less than theirs, they will realize that you are reacting somewhat, but not totally. That means that you are standing up for yourself, but are not as out of control as they are. That gives you an advantage.

If you lower your tone, that will be regarded as patronizing and can actually inflame the situation.

As you continue, you lower your tone, and reduce the speed. Then make your tone mellower, but keep it firm. Point out that they are raising their voice, which will probably make them do a double-take, then think again.

This tone-matching and tone-control will have a calming effect.

18

....

Don't shoot the messenger

No one loves the messenger who brings bad news.

Sophocles, *Antigone*

In my profession I have had to give bad news on many occasions. I have had to tell people about a diagnosis, a prognosis or even about the death of a relative or friend. It is never easy, yet when wearing the mantle of the profession it is not as difficult as it might otherwise be.

Bringing bad news

At some stage in life virtually everyone is going to have to be a messenger of gloom, a bearer of ill tidings. How bad that news is can vary from news that the neighbour's garage has been broken into, to telling someone that there has been a fatality somewhere.

As with all forms of talking that people dread, you can be prepared with just a little strategy.

ENERGY

This is another of the little acronyms that can be adapted to virtually all situations where you are going to have to deliver bad news.

- ► Express – *tell the person that you are sorry that you have some news to give. Be empathetic as you say it.*

  '*Mrs E – I am so sorry to have to tell you…*'
- ► News – *then the information is given.*

  '*I just heard that a supermarket trolley was pushed into your car.*'
- ► Explain – *here you explain the circumstances, and how you are the person that has the information.*

  '*A couple of young lads were messing about and they shoved it into the car park. I recognized your car and thought you must be in the supermarket.*'
- ► Reach out – *this is often going to be useful. When someone has received bad news they may feel shocked, and human contact at that time may help. Be careful, of course, that you only reach out if it is appropriate to do so. A hug may be acceptable for a relative or close friend, but not if there is a professional relationship. Do not do anything that could be deemed inappropriate. Certainly be wary of this with children. Reaching out to touch the back of their hand, putting a hand on a shoulder or extending a hand to shake may be more apt. Or no contact may be correct; in which case often showing the open hands palms upwards is a gesture of wishing to help.*

  '*Here let me take your bags out to the car.*'
- ► Gather information – *then you allow the person to take the news in and to express whatever feelings or information they want to. Gather it in, don't just nod and forget. There may be important information that you need to pass on to someone else.*

  '*Of course, I'll give your daughter a call and she can arrange everything with the garage.*'
- ► You – *this is the offer, again if appropriate, for them to get in touch if they wish or need.*

  '*You can always contact me, or call if it would help to talk.*'

The thing is that this strategy can be adapted to telling someone virtually any type of bad news.

Expressing sympathy

I talked about the stages of grief after bereavement in Chapter 14 on 'Making a speech'. In this day of emails, mobile phones and texting, people are able to send messages instantly to others when they have lost someone. Perhaps it is partly because of this that many folk dread the thought of actually going up to a grieving person to express their sympathy. Indeed, it is a common experience for many newly bereaved people to find acquaintances actually avoiding them rather than have to face the embarrassment of causing the grieving person to break down in front of them.

Yet expressing sympathy is an important human and feeling thing to do. It is a responsibility that should not be shirked.

EACH

The acronym that I find useful in this situation is the word EACH. It stands for the four things that you need to touch on.

- ▶ Express – *your sorrow at hearing the news. Be empathetic.*
- ▶ About – *it is entirely appropriate to ask about how the person passed away. Was it sudden, prolonged, an illness or an accident? This is something that the individual will probably want to talk about, albeit perhaps not for long if it is soon after the bereavement.*
- ▶ Coping – *ask how the person is coping. They may be managing very well. You can broaden the question out by asking if there is anyone at hand to help him or her to deal with things. Other members of the family, perhaps? Ask about the person's health as well.*
- ▶ Help – *an offer of help may go a long way towards helping the person. Just knowing that people are offering aid can be comforting. A simple 'Is there anything that I/we can do?'*

Whistle-blowing

This is a subject that is quite common in these days of increasing accountability. At one time in many occupations there was a tendency towards covering things up or, as people within organizations and professions would put it, protecting each other's backs.

Notorious cases in government, in politics, medicine, nursing, finance and sport have all shown that keeping quiet in such circumstances is no longer acceptable. When people's lives, welfare and their finances are being compromised then it is only correct that irregularities should be drawn to someone's attention. That may be a professional, occupational or even criminal matter.

The person who blows the whistle may find themselves in a difficult and hostile situation, with their job, health and even personal security being put at risk. It demands courage.

In the UK there is help for whistle-blowers in the form of the Public Interest Disclosure Act 1998, which is designed to protect them from vindictive employers. It prevents them from victimization and from dismissal.

You have to be very certain that there is something amiss. Whatever the organization that you work in, there will be some mechanism for dealing with this – an internal complaints procedure. This will usually mean contacting a line manager. If you ever find yourself in such a situation then you do need to be sure that you are taking the right action and that you are certain of your facts.

CERT

When you are concerned, quite appropriately since you have to be certain, think of the acronym CERT:

▶ Concern – *what exactly is your concern? Be able to define it. Is it a concern about someone's competence, a financial irregularity, or a safety issue?*

▶ Evidence – *this is very important. There must be precise and definite evidence; otherwise you open yourself up to a whole host of possible troubles, if your accusation is found to be without substance. You must not make unfounded allegations, but with hard evidence you are on solid ground. If you are just suspicious, that is another matter. In that case you might be as well sharing your suspicion with a colleague and you can both see whether there is evidence to proceed.*

▶ Reason – *what is your reason for voicing these concerns? Formulate it properly, don't just couch it in vague terms. You are concerned because the statistics indicate that lives are at risk here compared with the hospital down the road. The accounts show that there is unaccounted withdrawal of money. You must not be seen to be simply doing so on personal grounds.*

▶ Time – *how long has it been going on? This helps to back up the evidence and it also will show that you have had concerns for some time, that you have accumulated evidence and that you have made sure that the organization, profession, or public was being duped or put at risk.*

There is a call for you

Watson, come here; I want you.

Alexander Graham Bell, the very first telephone call in 1876

Mobile phone technology has made the world a very small place. You can instantly speak or text someone on the other side of the world at the press of a few buttons. How far the telephone has come since the day in 1876 when Alexander Graham Bell telephoned his assistant in another room.

While most people have grasped this technology and cannot imagine life without their mobile phone, there are a considerable number of people who have a real problem with any type of telephone and dislike using it at all. A small number even have a phobia – telephonophobia – which is so bad that they totally avoid ever speaking on the phone. It is usually part of a general social phobia, although some people have a specific telephonophobia. The main feature of the problem is avoidance behaviour.

What are you afraid of?

For people who have never experienced phobic fear, the thought of going out without their mobile in a pocket is unthinkable. They cannot imagine why anyone should fear such a useful part of modern life.

In fact, there seem to be three main reasons why people develop a telephonophobia:

1 *Some people have developed a belief that the phone or the electromagnetic field that emanates from the device can affect their health generally or their brain specifically. In this sense it can be part of a general hypochondriacal neurosis.*
2 *Others may have developed a form of magical thinking that is a form of obsessive-compulsive disorder, or OCD, in which they imagine that they will hear only bad news on the phone. If they answer it they will be tempting some outside force and something bad will happen to someone important to them as a result.*
3 *A greater number than the above two have a more general social anxiety and fear that they will not be able to talk, that the person on the other end will think them a fool and their vulnerability will be exposed.*

The net effect for them all is that they end up avoiding the phone, or they only ever use it after having first listened to the answerphone first. The result is that they rarely initiate a phone conversation, and they will tend not to make appointments and so forth.

If you recognize that you have a problem with the telephone that is like the first two examples above then you should make an appointment with your doctor, because these problems can definitely be helped. There is no need to deprive yourself of the benefits of the telephone.

··
Top Tip
The telephone is merely a tool to help you communicate.
··

Learning to love the telephone

As with virtually every human parameter, if you try to measure the enjoyment provided by the telephone you would find that you produce a bell-shaped graph. That is, the vast majority of people will have average enjoyment and form the bulk of the bell (to use a dreadful pun), while a small number at one extreme will be almost addicted to using it and another small amount will be totally phobic of it.

The people who love it have no problem talking on the phone and they can therefore skip the rest of this section. For those who would like to have less of a problem than they do, then read on.

ENJOY YOUR TELEPHONE VOICE

The first thing I would say is that you need to start listening to yourself. That is right; you need to get to know what you sound like. I have talked about this in Chapter 5 and I would recommend that you have a look back there after you have read this section.

Don't go back yet; I haven't finished. I want you to start to appreciate your phone voice!

You might wonder why that is, but, really, when you hear how good you sound that is half the battle. You will know that the person on the other end of the line will be enjoying the sound of your voice. Remember also that how you sound has a big impact.

I am sure that you will have answered the phone on occasions, assuming that you haven't always avoided using it, and been impressed by the sound of someone's voice. It may have startled you, for people do not always sound the same on the phone as they do face to face. That is inevitable, as there will be some distortions inherent upon speaking into a microphone. It is also the case that people unconsciously use a telephone voice.

Most people have answerphone capability on their land lines. To hear yourself simply phone your answerphone from another phone – land or mobile phone, it doesn't matter. Read a passage from a book or just leave yourself a message. Try to sound enthusiastic and interested.

Then have a listen. You may be surprised at how you sound if you have not done this before. Listen to it several times and appreciate its quality and tone. If you do not like it, then consider what you don't like about it, and think how you can modify it so that you do like it. And don't imagine that it is useless to try changing your voice. It isn't and in fact people do it all the time.

Indeed, I suggest that you cultivate the habit of doing so deliberately later on.

PICK UP THE PHONE

Direct confrontation is often a good thing to do with telephonophobia, because what can go wrong? The answer is nothing.

Nothing bad will happen to anyone as the result of you answering the phone. That is just magical thinking whereby things seem to be connected magically. It may be that once you did receive bad news by phone, but that was simply a chance occurrence.

Strategy

Next time the phone rings, don't wait for someone else to answer it, or for the call time to run out so that the phone stops ringing and goes onto answerphone. Pick it up, give your number and say, '… speaking.'

You have nothing to lose and you can cure yourself straight away.

REHEARSE WHAT YOU ARE GOING TO SAY

This is one of the repeated themes of this book and I make no apology for it. You should rehearse your talking.

Suppose you have to contact someone and give them a message or you want to order something, or even just make an appointment. Emails have made this easy and people switch on the computer and send off an email.

Do you do that? If you do, do you write the message straight off and send, or do you edit it? Do you write it and save it as a draft until you get it right, then send it? Those are forms of rehearsal, nothing more. They show a pride in the message that you want the other person to receive. There is nothing wrong with that, just as there is nothing wrong in rehearsing a telephone conversation.

Get your little talking notebook and jot down some notes. First write out a little patter for when you answer the phone. Something like:

'Hello, this is [your name]. How may I help you?'
That is bright and friendly. Don't just say, hello! That confuses the person on the other end and forces them to ask if they are speaking to the person they want, or it makes them ask to speak to you. If you then blandly say 'That's me' or 'Speaking!', it does not get things off to a crisp start. It makes you sound unenthusiastic or reticent. That is not what you want to sound like.

Then write down some patter for when you are making a call. Something like:

'Hello this is [full name] from [place of work, or the town you are speaking from], I would like to order/book/ speak to ...'
It is as simple as that. Have this in mind, or modify it so that it suits your new outgoing personality, and so that it is ready to slip off the tongue.

Now, suppose you want to order a commodity. Have the name of the commodity, its serial number, menu number, or whatever appertains to it from the information that you already have. Speak crisply and cheerfully.

You will be asked for details about how you will pay, possibly cash on delivery or, if you are happy to do so over the telephone, by credit card. Have that ready and speak clearly.

The other person will take all the information. There may be a pleasantry or two, and then you say thank you and goodbye.

Jot all of this down so that you have it in front of you. Now phone your answerphone from another phone, and then listen to how you sound. If you are not happy, try again. That is what rehearsal is all about.

Then try it in real life. You should find that it goes smoothly and that you feel a sense of achievement afterwards.

One thing to remember – do not get into the habit of echoing yourself. Some people do this, they end up saying goodbye, two or three times, each time getting lower until they put the phone down or switch off. It gives the impression of nervousness. That is something that you are going to leave behind.

Strategy

Rehearse a telephone order, then order a take-away meal.

TONE-MATCHING

We considered tone-matching in both Chapter 7 on 'How you look, act and say' and Chapter 17 on 'Talking to authority'. When you are on the telephone you will not have the advantage of seeing the other person so you cannot make any assessment about their body language or demeanour. The sound of their voice and their tone are the main things you have to go on apart from the words that they use.

You may find that the person on the other end of the phone is talking with quite a low tone that may indicate that they are more down in the dumps that you are. If you try lifting your tone, not your volume, you can lift their spirits.

It really is quite an interesting phenomenon and the more that you use the phone the more you can experiment to demonstrate to yourself how you can influence the conversation by using your voice, not just by talking.

GET A PHONE BUDDY

This is really a great thing to do. Having someone that you can phone up and talk to will help your confidence no end. It may be a relative or a friend. They may be surprised to find that out of the blue you, whom they never hear from by telephone, have started to make calls for a chat. If you can build that rapport so that either of you can phone the other to talk then you will find it benefits you enormously.

BE ENTHUSIASTIC

This is of fundamental importance. When you are on the phone aim to convey your enthusiasm and your interest in the person on the other end of the phone. If you know them, then use their name. If they have given you their name then use it repeatedly. Not in every sentence, of course, since that will come across as artificial, but certainly two or three times during the conversation.

DON'T BE AFRAID OF USING THE PHONE IN FRONT OF OTHER PEOPLE

Now do not misunderstand me, I do not mean that you should become gauche or rude and talk to other people during appointments, or when you are in a public place. That can mark you out as someone who is not considerate. What I mean is that you should not feel afraid of other people being present when you take a call.

Many people manifest part of a social anxiety by avoiding taking a call in an open area. They always make an excuse and take it in their office or by removing themselves from the area. That is a polite thing to do, but make sure that it is simple politeness that makes you operate this way. If it is fear of people seeing how you talk, or fear that you will look or sound silly, then you need to challenge this false belief that you hold.

The next time when you are called at work or in a social situation, assuming that it would be a reasonable thing to answer the call, then do so.

Do not imagine that people are watching and assessing you. They will be doing their best not to. So there is nothing to fear.

Strategy

Start making a habit of giving your phone number to friends. If you have a mobile phone then memorize the number. If you have to hunt for it on the phone then it indicates that you do not normally do this. By consciously remembering the number you are sending yourself the message that you are going to become a phone user.

20

Don't quote me – talking to the media

Giving an interview to the printed media, or talking on radio or television, all have their challenges and their rewards. If you are confident and know how to conduct yourself then you may even enjoy the experience.

I write a weekly newspaper column and am frequently asked for a comment on a health or any medical issue that has become topical. I have to say that my experience has been that the information that I have given has sometimes ended up in print in a very truncated or different manner from my original utterance. A journalist has information that they want to obtain, but the way that they transcribe that information will depend upon their particular spin on things. There is often no intention of altering your meaning; it is just what can happen.

I have given radio interviews and been interviewed on television in my capacity as a writer. In both mediums the same thing has happened. Fairly lengthy talks have been edited down, possibly for the best, but edited nonetheless to make them fit into a particular slot on a show.

If you find yourself being asked to speak to the media then you are as well to appreciate that you are not in control of the eventual material that will be read, heard or seen. That being the case you need to ensure that the things you do say are as clear, accurate and concise as possible.

Does it fill you with terror?

Some people are naturals in talking to and dealing with the media. I presume that you do not feel that you are, since this is a book aimed at helping you to talk when you feel tongue-tied and terrified. You should not allow yourself to get too anxious, however, since the limelight can be quite pleasant. Just look at the number of reality shows that fill television schedules and you will realize just how many people want to be viewed, recorded, listened to and admired on television. The reason all those people seek out such coverage is because they want to become celebrities. They want, as Andy Warhol put it, their 15 minutes of fame.

Assuming that you have read through the book you will know that the secret to all types of talking is to feel comfortable about yourself, to be well prepared and to have practised. If you have just opened the book up at this chapter and you want to find the secret to alleviate any anxiety before you appear on a TV interview tomorrow, then I recommend that you go back and read through Chapter 1 on 'Tongue-tied and terrified'. There are some immediate strategies that you can put into operation. Then read Chapter 7 on 'How you look, act and say'. Those combined with this chapter should give you some things to think about and some help, then it is a matter of good luck. Aim to enjoy the experience!

If your invitation is less anxiety-provoking than that, perhaps being an invite to do a few minutes on local radio in a week's time, then you have more room to manoeuvre. And you may have guessed it – a lot of that manoeuvring will involve preparation and practice.

Whenever you are asked to talk to the media consider the following points:

▶ *This is an opportunity.*
▶ *The media is an ally, not your enemy.*
▶ *The media wants a good story and you can give them it.*
▶ *It is your message that people want to hear.*
▶ *If you focus on the message rather than on your own fear there is no need to be afraid.*
▶ *As an actor play your part, so you have no reason to be afraid.*

Giving a newspaper interview

This should be the easiest of all. You are not being put in front of a camera, you are just being asked to tell your story or to give a view on something that you are presumably fairly expert upon.

When you receive the invitation, which could be by letter, email or phone call, begin by asking who the interviewer will be, whom he or she represents, and what the purpose of the interview is. You need to know what sort of angle they are planning, since there will be a slant that they want to put on it. This is something to be careful about if you are an expert on something that is in any way controversial or which people have strong views about. If you get the impression that you are being set up and you don't want to put your head in the lion's mouth, then you can politely refuse the interview.

On the other hand, perhaps it *is* something that you feel strongly about, in which case grasp it with both hands. If you are the expert, then believe in yourself and give them the information that you have.

If you are giving the interview as a private individual then that is one thing, of course. If you are the representative of an organization or society, make sure you have permission to give such an interview and whether your organization is happy for you to do so. It is best to check and if there is any doubt then decline.

If you feel that you need a little preparation to go over your information, then arrange an appointment to speak to the interviewer or for the interviewer to see you. It is quite acceptable to have a list of the topics or questions that they want to ask you about first.

Make some notes of the points that you want to make. This is the information that you consider to be the main part of the interview as opposed to the part that the interviewer may focus on. Ask if you can see the copy before it is produced. This really will depend upon the policy of the newspaper, magazine or journal.

Top Tip

Never assume that anything you say is off the record. The chances are that it will be on the record and that whereas you may have said 'don't quote me,' that is virtually a certain way of getting yourself quoted.

Radio interviews

The same basic questions arise. So you want to know the aim of the programme and the length of time that your slot will be.

Almost invariably the radio interviewer will be trying to put you at ease, unless you are going there in some sort of defensive role, such as to defend your company's position or role.

It is a good idea to listen to the programme before your interview if you can, so that you will get a sense of the way that interviews are slotted into the show, how the interviewer behaves and how they talk.

Do listen to the way that interviewers talk on radio shows. They will use their voices to convey things by altering volume, tone, pitch and speed of their voice. I have talked about tone-matching in several chapters, and this is quite an important thing to be aware of. Try to match the interviewer's tone, which will build empathy not only with him or her but, more importantly, between you and the listeners.

DON'T BE MONOTONE

This is good advice, which I give you from my own experience. Some years ago I was interviewed on a local BBC radio station about a book that I had written. It was about a subject that I was very interested in, yet when I listened to the recording I found the interview to be quite boring. The problem was, I realized, that I had a boring voice. Honestly, I did. The thing was that I had actually cultivated a boring monotone voice because I used hypnotherapy quite a lot in my medical practice. In order to induce a trance in people, one tries to make the voice as soporific as possible, and that means making it monotone. I had not realized, but I had done that on the radio.

The message is to be aware of one's tone and to give your voice enthusiasm and verve. Otherwise the listeners will fall into a deep, deep sleep!

PREPARE FOR AWKWARD QUESTIONS

Now you might wonder how you can do that, but the simple truth is that you will know what the awkward questions are likely to be. You will have come across them before and you will have an idea of how to answer them. A good radio journalist is going to ask those questions, so your job in preparation is to cover them and practise answering them.

It may be that you do not feel that you are able to answer such a question. If it is because you do not know the answer, then that is fine. Just be honest and say that you do not know the answer. It will become apparent if you are waffling.

Refusal to answer a question should be justified. Don't just say that it is not their business, or that you have no comment. Far better to say that you are not at liberty to answer.

Television

As I said, some people would give their eye teeth to get on television, so you should try to get excited about it. It is a terrific opportunity!

All of the points I made about print and radio invitations hold true with television as well. Very importantly make sure you find out whether you are going live or being pre-recorded. The pressure is off with a pre-recorded show, of course, but if it is live, then just be aware that what you say and do is what the audience are going to see.

Not very long ago I did an interview on a satellite TV programme called *Crime Writers*. I had watched several other crime writers being interviewed in a comfortable little sitting room by Rachael Harvey-Jones, a glamorous young interviewer. She was brilliant at putting her interviewees at ease, so I went feeling very excited.

And it was a super experience. The interview was about me, my writing and my latest book. I had ample opportunity to prepare a little book reading. I knew the questions she would ask and I was able to practise and rehearse in the comfort of my own home.

Although I was somewhat apprehensive beforehand, I managed to do it and I managed to keep myself calm. The preparation worked, my pre-interview visualizations worked and they were pleased with the interview. If I can do it, then so can you.

PRE-VISUALIZATION

This is a very useful thing to do in preparation before any television appearance. You simply prepare for it in your imagination. First, you get yourself into a relaxed state with progressive muscle relaxation.

Sit back in an easy chair or lie down somewhere that you will not be disturbed by a telephone or other interruptions. Take your shoes off so that the muscles are not restricted. Close your eyes and just tell yourself that you are going to relax all of your muscles. Tell yourself that as your muscles relax they will start to feel nice and heavy.

Now clench your fists tightly for a count of seven. As you do this focus your attention on the tightness in the hands, feeling it increase as you count to seven. Then suddenly let it go, and tell yourself that instead of tension there is now increasing relaxation in those muscles of the hand. And tell yourself that they will get even more relaxed as you count to fifteen.

Now clench your fists and this time also tense the muscles of your feet by trying to clench the toes. Do this for a count of seven, exactly as before. Then release the tension suddenly and let the relaxation deepen for a count of fifteen.

Now do it by clenching all of the muscles of your arms and of your legs, in exactly the same way. Tense for seven and relax for fifteen.

Then tense all of the muscles of all your limbs, clench the buttocks together and tense the stomach muscles and your neck and face muscles. Screw your eyes tightly closed as you count to seven, and then release suddenly and relax for fifteen.

Then tell yourself that your muscles are now going to relax totally and that they will continue to relax and will feel more comfortable when you stop. Now imagine that a wave of relaxation is moving all the way up over your body from your feet, up your legs, up your back and chest to your neck. Let that feeling pass down both arms and up your neck to your head, relaxing all of the muscles as it moves up over the top of your head and down over your face. Tell yourself that you will enjoy that for a minute of so.

Then you tell yourself that there is a television screen in front of you and that you can see it in your mind's eye. You can hear it and it is as if you were actually watching it.

Then you see the television programme that you are going to be on, complete with all of the TV jingles, the presenter and the studio backdrop. Watch it and enjoy it, feeling how pleasantly relaxing it is. Then the presenter is speaking about you, giving you a build-up. And then the camera is on you and you see yourself facing the camera and smiling.

And the interview is off to a start. You are asked the questions you anticipate. You reply, adding humour if appropriate. You empathize with the interviewer, using tone-matching of your voice. The reactions are good. The time is passing until the interview is over.

You find it hard to believe that it was over so soon. You enjoyed it. You can't wait to have another one.

Then you allow yourself just to enjoy the pleasant relaxing feeling of success. If you want you can drift off to sleep, from which you will eventually awake feeling relaxed and confident about the forthcoming interview. Or you can tell yourself that you are going to count from one to seven and that with each number you will feel more and more alert until at seven you are fully alert and raring to go having enjoyed the experience.

This is an excellent thing to do every day in the period leading up to the interview. Each time you do it you will feel more and more confident until the interview itself comes and you prepare to enjoy yourself, basking in the new-found pleasure of television.

A FEW PRE-TV TIPS

Television is all about appearance, so take note of the following snippets.

The camera puts on weight
It does, really. About half a stone in fact, so you may wish to consider that. On the other hand, if you are comfortable in yourself that is fine.

Dress appropriately
Viewers do make judgements about the state of people's dress and their general appearance. Make sure that your hair is groomed, your hands are clean and your nails well trimmed.

Choose your clothing well. Bright colours are OK, but it is best to avoid stripes or jarring patterns.

Make sure everything fits well. Men should not show flesh between socks and the bottoms of their trousers, women should be wary of showing too much skin if they wish to be taken seriously.

Sit properly
You should sit comfortably, but with a good posture. That means sit up straight, don't cross your legs inelegantly. Do not slouch.

Do not fidget
You must be careful of making inappropriate gestures. The camera will magnify all unnecessary gestures and mannerisms and you may end up looking like someone trying to catch invisible flies.

Stay in the present
It is easy to lose concentration in the unreal world of a studio and get distracted by the movements of the cameramen. If two or more of you are present then do not just focus only on what you are saying and contributing. You may be asked to comment on what another interviewee just said. Show interest in the interviewer and the others present.

Smile appropriately

It is good to be interactive, and use the smiles that you have practised making before. Be sure that any such smiling is appropriate, however.

Punctuality

If you are invited onto radio or television then do ensure that you know where the studio is and that you make arrangements to arrive there punctually. Better still arrive early so that you can get yourself prepared and relaxed before the programme. If you are going on television then you may or may not be offered some wardrobe grooming. If not, then do take advantage of the toilet facilities and check hair and general appearance.

Speak with your interviewer

This really should be up to the interviewer, but try to ensure that you have the opportunity to have a quick run-through of the slot. You want to be clear what is going to be asked and that you are not going to be asked anything embarrassing or anything that is unexpected. You are within your rights to ask that certain things be placed out of bounds of the interview. Most presenters and interviewers will respect your wishes, unless you are going on a programme that is of an investigative nature or where you are in a defensive role, in which case a grilling is possible.

You can still decide whether you want to be interviewed or not.

Stimulants

Some people are tempted to relax by using alcohol beforehand. Do not do this. Alcohol does relax you, but it does so by damping down inhibitory neurones. It is not a stimulant at all, but a depressant of nerve function. The danger is that it will make you too uninhibited and also less sharp mentally.

21

....

Afterwords – keep talking!

There is an old adage that success begets success. The fact that you picked up a book about talking in the first place is suggestive that you have needed help with some aspect of talking. The likelihood is that some engagement or potential talking occasion was troubling you and that you felt you needed help. It is my fond hope that within these pages you will have found that there is enough information and strategies to help you through it.

Perhaps the occasion has already passed and you have chalked it up as another thing done on the list of goals in your life. If so, then I would urge you not to leave matters as they are, but to forge ahead with your new-found skills. It is good to talk and I fully imagine that you will have felt a thrill of achievement as you sailed through the occasion or event.

Practice might not make perfect, but it does hold you in good stead. Like any other human activity, however, if you let the practice slip, then the skill that you achieved will start to dwindle. Not only does practice help you to raise your level of attainment, but it helps you to maintain it until you achieve expert status.

So rather than leave the book on the shelf, do keep delving into it and keep practising the techniques I have gone through. Use the strategies in all of the different situations and add new ones that you will discover for yourself. Each new success will reinforce the last, each one making the next event easier in prospect. The result is that instead of anticipatory anxiety you will experience only excitement and impatience to get on with the job.

Practice changes the way the brain works

If you want a job doing properly, ask a professional to do it. That's good advice, isn't it? Whether it is an electrical job, a computer repair or a plumbing problem, a trained professional seems able to just come in, diagnose the problem and fix it relatively easily. It doesn't matter how difficult the problem is, they seem to be able to solve it in a fraction of the time that you can. It's just practice, you might say. Well, that is true of course, but it is more complex than that. When someone becomes an expert at something their brain actually starts to work differently when they are applying it to that area.

You can see this in virtually every occupation. After a time people become adept. With experience they become skilled. A stage beyond that and they become so expert that they may feel that they can perform certain tasks with their eyes closed and their hands tied behind their backs. It is as if they develop a sixth sense. You will have heard of doctors making a snap diagnosis, police officers sniffing a rat or sensing a crime, and journalists just knowing when there is a story to be covered. Singers know how to sing a song just right and practised talkers can just open their mouths and let their eloquence work its magic.

In recent research in Japan a team involved in cognitive brain mapping studied a group of professional Shogi players and compared them with group of amateur players. (Shogi is the Japanese form of chess.) Both groups were shown various board patterns and asked to make a sequence of rapid moves.

They found that there were two marked differences in the way that the brains of the two groups functioned. First, the professionals instantly activated parts of their brains called the 'precuneus' in the parietal lobes, under your crown. Secondly, when forced to make quick moves the experts activated a structure called the 'caudate nucleus' in their basal ganglia.

These brain findings correspond with what we think of as intuition, or just good old-fashioned know-how. You have to train the brain to become expert in your field, but once you have developed know-how, your brain just does it without thinking.

The same thing holds for all aspects of talking. Practise and keep practising your talking in various situations and you will lose your nerves, your brain will move to expert level and you will no longer feel tongue-tied and terrified.

Everyone may just think that you kissed the Blarney Stone.

Bibliography

Bandler, R. and Grinder, J. *Frogs into Princes* (Real People Press, 1979; Eden Grove Editions, 1990)

Darwin, C. *The Expression of the Emotions in Man and Animals* (1872; Digireads.com Publishing, 2009)

Frankl, V. *The Doctor and the Soul: From Psychotherapy to Logotherapy* (Souvenir Press, 2004).

Hall, E.T. *The Hidden Dimension* (Anchor Books, 1990)

Lane, C. *Shyness: How Normal Behavior Became a Sickness* (Yale University Press, 2007)

Morris, D. *The Naked Ape: A Zoologist's Study of the Human Animal* (Jonathan Cape, 1967)

Morris, D. *Manwatching* (Jonathan Cape, 1977)

Stone, H. *and Stone, S. Embracing your Inner Critic* (Harperone, 1993)

Slater, E, and Roth, M. *Clinical Psychiatry* (Bailliere Tindall, 1977)

Index